Theme Immersion

Theme Immersion

Inquiry-Based Curriculum in Elementary and Middle Schools

MARYANN MANNING
GARY MANNING
ROBERTA LONG

HEINEMANN
Portsmouth, New Hampshire

HEINEMANN
A division of Reed Elsevier Inc.
361 Hanover Street   Portsmouth, NH 03801-3912
Offices and agents throughout the world

Every effort has been made to contact the copyright holders for permission to reprint borrowed material where necessary. We regret any oversights that may have occurred and would be happy to rectify them in future printings of this work.

Library of Congress Cataloging-in-Publication Data
Manning, Maryann Murphy.
   Theme immersion : inquiry-based curriculum in elementary and
middle schools / Maryann Manning, Gary Manning, Roberta Long.
        p.   cm.
   Includes bibliographical references.
   ISBN 0–435–08806–8
   1. Education, Elementary—United States—Curricula.   2. Middle
schools—United States—Curricula.   3. Elementary school teaching—
United States.   4. Language experience approach in education—
United States   5. Interdisciplinary approach in education—
United States.   I. Manning, Gary L.   II. Long, Roberta.   III. Title.
LB1570.M365   1994
372.19—dc20   93–43027
                                                          CIP

Editor: Philippa Stratton
Production: J.B. Tranchemontagne
Text and Cover design: Jenny Jensen Greenleaf
Photos in Chapters 1 through 8: Charles Nesbitt
Cover photo and photos in Chapter 9: Rob Nelson

Printed in the United States of America on acid-free paper
     99   98   97   96   95   94   HP   7   6   5   4   3   2   1

Contents

Acknowledgments

To acknowledge all the friends and colleagues who made some contribution to the publication of this book is impossible. The acknowledgments would be as long as the book itself. Let us simply give a big "thank you" to all of them and mention those who helped us in the actual writing of the book. Our heartfelt thanks go first of all to the following teachers and their students, who welcomed us into their classrooms to observe and participate in the implementation of their various theme immersions: Ginny Blackburn, Jody Brewer, Sonia Carrington, Ann Dominick, Naomi Goss, Ginny Hart, Amanda Kutz, Linda Maxwell, Gayle Morrison, Sherry Parrish, Debra Rust, Ann Stevens, and Phillip Westbrook. We also want to thank the school principals for their support and the parents for their permission to use both the photographs of their children and their children's work.

It is a pleasure to thank the photographers, Charles Nesbitt and Rob Nelson, for their hard work and consummate professionalism. Charles took the photographs for Chapters 1 through 8, and Rob those for the photographic essay in Chapter 9. Their photographic skill and sincere interest in our work added immeasurably to the book.

We are especially indebted to Pat Broderick and Philippa Stratton. Pat, vice-president and editor of *Teaching K–8*, always responded quickly and willingly to our numerous requests for help throughout the writing of the manuscript and guided us in the development of Chapter 9. Philippa, editor-in-chief at Heinemann, consistently provided us with gentle support and superb guidance. Without her, the book would not have been completed.

We should also like to thank fellow author Bobbi Fisher for her insightful suggestions for improving the manuscript and our longtime friend Dottie Thompson for her critique, from the perspective of a class-room teacher, of the various manuscript drafts. And, finally, we are deeply grateful to family members Delbert Long, husband of Roberta, whose critical acumen helped us clarify many of our ideas; and Marilee Roberta Manning, the teenage daughter of the Mannings, whose patience and love were a source of inspiration and encouragement to all of us.

Prologue

JEROME: How did he get poor?

JUNE: I think some people are always that way and some people get that way.

JEROME: But what about him? What was he? Was he all the time poor or just now?

JUNE: Well, he didn't exactly say, but he said he had a family. A little girl like me. He said he once had a real house.

MARTHA: Then he must have not always been without a home.

ALLEN: Does he have health insurance and stuff like that?

AMY: I don't know, but I'll bet he doesn't.

ALLEN: How can we get to know what really happened to him, I mean, why is he on the street with no food? How many old newspapers does he put over himself to keep warm?

This dialogue occurred in a fifth-grade classroom after Amy told a group of classmates what she had experienced at the Firehouse Shelter in downtown Birmingham, Alabama, the night before. She had gone with her father to help serve food to the homeless men at the shelter, which is sponsored by the United Way. Amy, age eleven, didn't know a lot about homelessness, but she was disturbed about what she had seen. Although she had only been to the shelter once, she quickly became the class expert on homelessness, and other class members besieged her with questions about her experience.

Allen raised his voice as he said, "It isn't really cold yet. What good would newspapers be when it gets cold? What if it snows? The newspapers would just get wet and probably freeze."

Laurie Wall, the teacher, noticed the seriousness on the faces of the small group surrounding Amy. The students all talked at once as they tried to explain what Amy had told them. Laurie asked the class if they wanted to hear about Amy's experience.

AMY: I didn't even want to go with my dad last night but my mom had some meeting at church, so I had to go since they won't let me stay alone at night. My dad goes downtown to this place that used to be a fire station. When we went in, we passed men who had old clothes on and who just stood or sat outside waiting to get in to eat.

She went on to tell how she had helped butter bread for the meal that was served to the men. Amy told in great detail about how everything was done at the shelter, what the men ate, and that only thirty-five of the men who were waiting outside got to sleep in the shelter that night.

Several students commented on homeless people they had seen on downtown streets. Allen told about those he had seen in Philadelphia when he visited his uncle. Several others told about what they had learned from television and from listening to people talk.

Laurie wasn't surprised at the reaction of the class because these kids had already shown interest in social issues. They had visited a nursing home up the street and made favors for the Thanksgiving trays of the residents. She asked the class, "Is homelessness something that interests you? In other words, do you want to really delve into it for a couple of weeks?" There were shouts of "Yes," and she sensed the sincerity of the students.

Thus, a new "theme immersion," an intensive, in-depth study of one topic, was born, but this one was unlike any theme from a book or curriculum guide; it was unique to Laurie's class. A special chemistry was created in this community of learners. The ingredients were the interests and prior knowledge of each class member and of their teacher, the resources available to the class at school and in the community, and Laurie's ability to guide and nurture the theme immersion.

Fortunately, the class was just winding down on a theme immersion about Canada, a district-mandated topic. Laurie had planned to follow the Canadian study with one on Mexico, but she knew there was plenty of time left in the year to study everything in the required school district curriculum. Even though she loved studying Mexico and piñatas at Christmastime, she decided she couldn't pass up an opportunity for a unique theme. And the children were filled with energy and ready to burst.

Here was a topic she didn't know much about, but it interested her. She couldn't wait to learn from her students, and she knew that her own excitement would spill over to them as they began the study. There was much to do, but they had already overcome the most difficult hurdle. The students were interested, and their interest had originated with them.

Laurie hasn't always taught this way. There was a time not so many years ago when she could have been characterized as a traditional teacher: She was conscientious, she cared about her students, and she knew her subject matter, yet she taught subject by subject, although she recognized that this was sometimes boring for her and for her students. In the last several years, she has evolved from being a teacher bound to textbooks and following school district guidelines to the letter, to being a whole language teacher teaching in an interdisciplinary manner. Now she uses the model of theme immersion as a way of making content exciting for her students and at the same time developing their language arts skills. She also meets district expectations in the content areas.

Laurie has plenty to do to prepare the homelessness theme immersion, but it's exciting. She has to engage the students in planning the study, assist them in finding sources of information, help them determine the important issues for discussion as they exchange different points of view, and aid them in deciding how to communicate what they learn.

For at least two hours a day over the next three weeks, students worked on the topic of homelessness. They recorded their research findings and wrote down their concerns and feelings about homelessness. They read books about homelessness, poverty, and related topics. They called their congressional representatives' offices to ask for information about congressional hearings. They couldn't wait to write letters to the various agencies for the homeless and eagerly awaited the responses. In the lunch line and during lunch, they argued about proposed solutions to the problems of the homeless. In the evenings, they talked to their parents and neighbors to find out what they knew about the homeless and how they felt about the problem.

Although students still had regular math class, they practiced math as they compiled statistics on the number and condition of the homeless from newspapers, interviews with social workers, and government agencies. Health education was a major topic as they explored the lack of physical and mental health care. Drug education was another major topic, since many homeless people seem to have drug problems. Laurie was surprised by the children's arguments about whether or not needles should be provided for drug users. Some students thought needles should be provided in order to minimize the AIDS epidemic, and some thought they shouldn't.

One afternoon during the study, Laurie read Eve Bunting's *Fly Away Home* aloud to the class. The ensuing discussion revealed the students' sensitivity to the problems of the homeless. Laurie wished some of the adults she knew were as socially conscious about the issues surrounding the homeless as these fifth graders were.

The enthusiasm of this class was contagious; other teachers and students wanted to learn about the homeless and do something to help. The whole school became involved in a food drive for the shelter where Amy had gone with her father. Allen's Boy Scout troop distributed flyers to every house and apartment in the community describing a Saturday used clothing drive they were setting up. The Scouts asked that used clothes be placed in bags on porches on a specific Saturday; troop members then picked up the bags and took them to several shelters in town. Class members became social activists. They wrote letters to the city council, the mayor, and the newspaper. One of these letters was actually published. They asked church and community organizations about their respective contributions to solving the problem of the homeless.

Students expressed their new knowledge in several ways. One group wrote an opinion piece and distributed it throughout the school community. Jerome painted a water color to depict the hopeless feelings of many homeless people, and Amy wrote a poignant poem about the men she saw at the shelter.

The impact of the theme immersion on the lives of these fifth graders was tremendous. Perhaps some of them will become adults who work toward solutions to the difficult problems plaguing their country and the world.

Becoming a Theme Immersion Teacher

Theme immersion is an in-depth study of a topic, issue, or question. Students engage in the planning of the study with the teacher. Together they find resources for information, determine the important issues for discussion, and decide how to communicate their learning. Specific content evolves as a TI progresses; some students become interested in new topics as a result of their study and begin to explore areas that may not be directly related to the original topic, issue, or question. The role of the teacher is not to impose or control ideas but to be an active member of the community of learners.

We liken theme immersion to a giant oak tree. The roots represent the theoretical foundations. The trunk represents theme immersion. As students and the teacher plan cooperatively, areas of study emerge and the tree grows. How many branches the tree has and how large the tree becomes depend on several things: the number of subtopics and related issues that can be studied, the degree of interest shown by students and teacher, and the amount of available information. Some TIs seem like pine trees on a wind-swept hill with only a few branches, others like fruit trees whose heavy-laden branches hang close to the ground.

Recently, Sharon, a third-grade teacher, told us, "I read your article on TI [Manning and Manning, 1991], and at first I thought I was already doing theme immersion, but then I realized that you were talking about something very different." Sharon went on to say that she had spent years developing her units. She described her wide collection of trade books and other resources. But after reading the article, she realized that a major difference between her units and our description of a TI was that she remained in complete control of all aspects of the units: *she* selected the topic, *she* chose all the materials and activities, and *she* decided each unit's direction and outcome. Before our conversation ended, it was clear that Sharon had decided to become a TI teacher, to involve her students in all aspects of an in-depth study of a topic, issue, or question.

We'd like to think that Sharon will develop into a masterful TI teacher like those we describe in this book. The TI teachers depicted here are themselves continuous learners seeking new and better ways to support children's learning. They work hard every day to make their teaching more closely reflect their knowledge about instructional content, about the teaching-learning process, and about how children learn. These teachers view themselves as lifelong learners and actively engage in reading for pleasure and for information. They realize the power of writing both for themselves and for their students. They want students to have a real voice in the classroom. They want schools filled with children who not only *can* read, write, and think but *do* read, write, and think. They want their students to have a positive attitude toward learning and to become lifelong learners who care about their world and want to make it a better place.

While there is no "magic" approach to make learning in school more meaningful and relevant, theme immersion teachers are improving the quality of education in schools by helping their students make connections between their activities in the classroom and the real world of today and tomorrow. These teachers are successful because they base their teaching on sound theory. Like them, we, too, have strong reasons for believing in theme immersion.

Our Journey to Theme Immersion

We have each been involved in education for about thirty years, although our experiences have been very different. Maryann taught for two years in a K–8 one-room country school and for five years in two very small high schools in rural Nebraska; she then spent five more years as a fourth-grade teacher in Omaha, Nebraska. Roberta taught at the elementary level in faraway places like Nepal, Indonesia, Thailand, Czechoslovakia, Germany, and the former Soviet Union. Gary, the administrator in the group, taught the elementary grades in Cook and Ralston, Nebraska, and then served for several years as an elementary school principal in Ralston, Nebraska, and as a director of elementary education in the Nebraska State Department of Education.

Although we are from different parts of the country and have vastly different educational backgrounds and experiences, the three of us brought to our teaching at the University of Alabama at Birmingham some very similar beliefs. All of us, for example, had been touched by John Dewey during our graduate school days. It was Dewey who first sparked our serious thinking about what the teaching-learning process at its best should be. Dewey's writings have continued to help us think imaginatively about this process.

Recently, in reviewing some of Dewey's (1910; 1915; 1938) seminal work on education, we realized that many of his beliefs are as relevant for education today as they were during his lifetime. Five of them in particular provide a strong underpinning for theme immersion. First, Dewey stressed that the curriculum should not be a series of subjects isolated from the everyday lives of children and young people. As he wrote, "careful observation of interests is of the utmost importance for the educator. . . . Only through the continual and sympathetic observation of childhood's interests can the adult enter into the child's life and see what it is ready for, and upon what material it could work most readily and fruitfully" (1910, pp. 14-15). We agree that the teacher must become his or her own curriculum maker. Second, in an ideal school curriculum, what should be stressed is not a "succession of studies" but the "development of new attitudes towards, and new interests in, experiences" (1910, p. 13). Third, teachers must instill in children the desire to learn throughout their lives. Fourth, students and teachers must work together cooperatively and learn from each other. Fifth, teachers must encourage children to do their part to make the world a better place.

Jean Piaget (1963; 1964) has also influenced our thinking. During the last few years we have begun to understand the importance of his theory for educational practice. In the early eighties, Constance Kamii, who had been one of Piaget's research fellows, came to our university. She conducted seminars on Piaget's theory and shared her own research on how children construct mathematical knowledge. Moreover, she helped us and continues to guide us in understanding how Piagetian theory applies to language learning and learning in general.

We have found that four of Piaget's basic principles provide strong theoretical support for theme immersion: First, students construct their own knowledge from within rather than have it imposed on them from some external source. Second, social interaction contributes significantly to students' construction of knowledge. Individuals think critically when they defend their own ideas while trying to resolve other points of view. Third, risk-taking and making mistakes are critical to learning. Finally, moral and intellectual autonomy are important educational goals.

Piaget was interested in explaining how human beings come to know. His research is an important source of help for us in our quest to find ways to support children's learning.

The sixties and early seventies in America were tumultuous times not only for young people but for us as educators. Young people were dissatisfied with the way society was going, and we were dissatisfied with the way education seemed to be going: long checklists of skills in all curriculum areas; reading skills continua; standardized testing; division of subject matter; the list goes on and on. To us, college teachers of language arts, this chopped-up approach to learning just didn't make sense. We became whole language educators, though we didn't have a label at the time. We read the works of psycholinguists such as Frank Smith (1971), who taught us that students learn to read and write in the process of doing so, and Kenneth Goodman (1970; 1986), who taught us that reading is a process of active interaction with print, not the learning of a series of isolated skills. Through Yetta Goodman's (1978; 1987) writings we became "kid watchers": we had a new window through which to examine children's thinking and new ideas for assessing and evaluating children's written language development.

We became familiar with L. S. Vygotsky's (1978; 1987) concept of the "zone of proximal development." According to Vygotsky, children have two developmental levels, an actual developmental level determined by things the child can do on his or her own and a potential level determined by what the child can do with the guidance of an adult or in collaboration with more capable peers. Vygotsky called the distance between these two levels the "zone of proximal development." Acknowledging the existence of these two levels sends a powerful message to teachers, because an essential feature of teaching and learning is the creation of the zone of proximal development. If we want children to work in the zone of proximal development, we must create classroom conditions that provide opportunities for a great deal of classroom interaction and collaboration.

Gordon Wells's (1986) research provides yet another foundation stone for our theoretical framework. Basing his conclusions on fifteen years of longitudinal research into how children learn language and how they use language to learn, Wells shows that children are active makers of meaning and suggests how adults can help them learn. He reminds us that "starting where a child is" doesn't mean starting where he or she is according to some standardized test, it means understanding each child's "mental model of the world" and his or her current interests. Only then can the teacher contribute to the child's further learning. One reason many children are not successful in school, he suggests, is that we can't "start where the child is" when there is an imposed, preplanned curriculum in which the child has no voice and which does not take into account the needs and interests of individual children.

Wells proposes a collaborative model of education—a partnership between students and teacher—in which the teacher, as the more skilled and knowledgeable of the partners, serves as the master who provides guidance "to an apprentice, who utilizes that guidance in the pursuit of his or her chosen goal, the value of which is appreciated by both of them" (1986, p. 120). Influenced by the ideas of Dewey and reports from teachers who have been successful in using a collaborative model of education, Wells proposes that we organize instruction around broad themes. Theme immersion allows for negotiation between students and teacher, for individual choice within a broad topic, and for opportunities to work with and learn from each other.

Our own research and writing, and that of other whole language educators and researchers such as Dorothy Watson (1987), Brian Cambourne (1988), and Donald Graves (1983), have contributed further underpinnings to theme immersion. Whole language relates to the total curriculum, not just the language curriculum. Ken Goodman and his colleagues describe whole language as "curricula that keep language whole and in the context of its thoughtful use in real situations" (1987, p. 6). In TI classrooms, learning is kept whole: children practice literacy skills as they engage in meaningful pursuits related to the selected theme and as they prepare and communicate their learning to others.

The work of Dewey, Piaget, Vygotsky, Wells, and whole language advocates supports the idea that the classroom is a community and that the teacher is a guide and an agitator of intellectual activity. Their ideas also support the notion that classroom activities should be authentic and should resemble the real world as much as possible.

Theme immersion enables us to put into practice our beliefs about teaching and learning.

We believe that

- The TI classroom is one in which a community of learners work together.
- The teacher is guide, facilitator, and co-learner in the community.
- Children's engagement in social interaction is essential to the learning process.
- Student choice and interest are important in all aspects of the curriculum.
- Intellectual and moral autonomy is fostered as students help each other become good decision makers.
- All human beings should be respected and diversity valued.

Role of the Theme Immersion Teacher

A major difference between a traditional unit and a TI is the way the teacher perceives her role in the classroom. Teachers realize that they don't just assign tasks and dispense information; they support students as students explore answers to their own questions. Teachers don't motivate students by dangling grades and rewards in front of them but by nurturing intrinsic motivation. They know that students' desire to learn is like a log in the fireplace—it needs the right conditions in order to burn. TI teachers provide fuel in the form of good questions, good resources, and sufficient time to research and discuss questions.

Instead of following a predetermined guide, a TI teacher makes her own curriculum decisions. She knows that her students are learning from the inside out—that they construct their own knowledge based on their prior knowledge. When we taught in a more traditional way, we focused on teaching students the skills and concepts listed in the curriculum. TI teachers know that if students read widely, talk about their understandings, and then share what they know, they will learn more than if they had specific content spelled out for them. What each student learns, however, will be different because of that student's interests and prior knowledge.

Topics

For students to become immersed in a topic, they must be interested in it. Our challenge as teachers is to capitalize upon and expand these interests, and to have each child working in his or her zone of proximal development. Probably none of the students in Amy's class would have said they wanted to study the homeless if interviewed about their interests, but once Amy shared her concern, they were eager to learn more.

A topic should be *important* to the classroom community and to society at large. In addition, it must be *broad* enough in scope to help students develop an awareness of the interconnectedness of the world. For example, crime in one neighborhood is usually tied to the crime problem in a city, state, nation, and the world. Students and teachers who are interested in saving a historic train station in their community soon begin thinking about the preservation of landmarks throughout the country. As students become interested in the welfare of residents of a local nursing home, they write letters, make decorations for meal trays, and volunteer to help on Saturday; in this way they begin to see aspects of aging in a broader context. Topics such as the care of the aged touch their concern for other human beings and help them expand their connections to others during a TI.

The exploration that is intrinsic to a TI must present opportunities for nurturing an understanding of and a respect for cultural diversity. Since social interaction among students is an integral part of a TI classroom and since students' opinions and views are valued by the teacher and their fellow classmates, students hear different points of view about issues such as cultural diversity. They reexamine their own egocentric views and become more objective in their thinking because they are challenged to consider what is best for all citizens.

TI topics should have the potential for disagreement. There is an old saying that goes something like this: "Everyone loves a good fight." We don't necessarily agree, but we do think that we learn more when we dig in our heels and take sides on an issue. Being a little hot around the collar as you disagree with others often causes you to think more deeply about your own point of view: while researching one side of an issue, you may encounter information that runs counter to your point of view; you then have to concede that you were wrong or continue looking for supporting evidence to prove your side of the argument.

Not long ago, we heard a student discussion in a fifth-grade class during a TI on nuclear waste. The class had undertaken the study when a local newspaper published a story about the nuclear dump sites in the state. Passions were running high: Some students thought the number of people with cancer would increase. Others thought the sites would help the economy by creating jobs for unemployed citizens. Only a few students felt the nuclear waste would not hurt anyone. One boy said, "Why don't we send all the nuclear waste to Mississippi?" Initially, some students agreed with him, but soon the rest of the class started sounding like delegates to the United Nations protecting Mississippi and the world.

Activities

The activities in a TI are not gimmicky or glitzy. There are no word puzzles or cute games There are no worksheets or set routines, such as answering all the questions on all chapters in a textbook. Rather, the emphasis of a TI is on exploring answers to questions through reading in a wide variety of books, both fiction and nonfiction, getting information from other people, experiencing through community trips, demonstrations, simulations, role playing, and so on. Students work in committees and discuss issues. After they have gathered their information and clarified and elaborated on their thinking, they express their knowledge in any number of ways.

Evaluation

TI evaluation procedures are qualitative rather than quantitative in nature. There are no pre-tests, post-tests, end of unit tests, or "bubble in the circle" exercises. Instead, teachers and students evaluate participation in the process of the TI: "Were you a contributing member of your committee?" "How effective were you in finding answers to your questions?" Samples of individual student work are placed in student portfolios, and committee and class work is displayed in the classroom and in school hallways. Even when TI teachers are required to give letter grades or percentages, they look for ways to involve students in the evaluation process. They consider a wide variety of activities in determining grades, not just the correct answers on tests.

Differences Between Theme Immersions and Theme Units

There are distinct differences between theme units and theme immersion. When we used theme units years ago, we used a specific topic to teach subjects and skills. We identified the concept and the generalizations we wanted to teach and often tried to force all areas of the curriculum into the unit. There is no doubt in our minds that theme units are better than isolated subject area techniques, but there are some significant differences between the traditional model of units and themes and theme immersion. These differences are outlined in the following chart:

	Traditional Units	Theme Immersion
Topic Selection	Selected by teacher or dictated by the curriculum	Negotiated between teacher and student
Content	Designated by topic: animals, weather, soil erosion	Focused on broad issues: endangered species, homelessness, civil rights
	Content pre-selected	Content evolves
Cultural Diversity	Selected cultures studied at designated period	Integrated into classroom environment and part of all activities
Theoretical Framework	Behaviorism	Constructivism
Skill Development	Skills specific to content areas	Skills develop in the process of use as students explore a particular question
Role of Teacher	Determines, plans, and directs most activities	Guides students' learning and serves as member of community; serves as a model learner
Learning Activities	Preplanned by teacher	Self-selected and cooperatively planned by students and teacher
	Activities not necessarily about content	Activities related to integral aspects of content—no artificial connections

Who Should Use Theme Immersions?

Whole language teachers are successful using TIs because their beliefs are compatible with those that underlie theme immersion. Teachers who may not call themselves whole language teachers but believe that reading and writing are processes rather than only content to be learned, and accept the tenets of Dewey, Piaget, Vygotsky, and Wells are active candidates. These teachers are probably already incorporating many aspects of TI in their teaching.

TIs find an ideal setting in a self-contained classroom, but they can be used effectively in a team teaching structure and in departmentalized settings. In this book, you will get to know several teachers, at different grade levels in different teaching situations, whose students are immersed in TIs for much of the day.

Theme Immersion Topics

2

No aspect of theme immersion is more crucial than the selection of the right topic. A topic should be of importance and interest to as many members of the learning community as possible. It must be something worthy of all the time and energy that will be invested in it. In the final analysis, the teacher must use her knowledge and understanding of the subject matter and of human learning in making decisions about topic choices, including those topics that are selected by students.

Who Selects the Topic?

In our dream school, the students and the teacher are ecstatic about all the topics that are studied. In reality, though, it is seldom possible for everyone to be equally interested in any particular theme. More success will be achieved, however, if all voices are represented in the selection of a topic and if there is ample latitude for pursuing various aspects of the theme. Some topics are chosen by the students, others by the teacher; sometimes a topic may flow naturally from a shared class experience. Then, of course, there are topics that may be mandated by the school system or state department of education. We will discuss and give examples of each of these in this chapter.

Student-Selected Theme Immersions

Most teachers enjoy following the natural interests of their students and find student topics to be some of the most exciting. Student selection can take place through a formal procedure or informally through a class discussion, or it may emerge from a shared experience.

In formal selection, an initial step is a topic brainstorming session in which students make a list of every topic they say they want to study. The group discusses the topics and, where possible, combines several to make them more comprehensive. Then the class votes, narrowing the list until consensus is reached, which helps to assure the interest of most of the students.

Students are interested in hundreds of topics. In one fifth-grade classroom, Bobbie, the teacher, asked students about topics they wanted to study and led a discussion about issues affecting the world today. She mentioned the example of the inequality of the races in South Africa to get students' thinking started. These students were already active in watching news programs on television and discussing contemporary issues with their parents and others, and they were able to brainstorm the following list in less than an hour:

Affordable housing	Immigration laws
AIDS	Inflation
Armed conflicts	Legal equality
Chemical weather control	Nuclear proliferation
Deforestation	Political conflicts
Deterioration of ozone layer	Pollution
Disease control	Problems of the aging
Disposal of toxic waste	Religious conflicts
Economic inequality	Sex discrimination
Energy consumption	Space exploration
Euthanasia	Technology and unemployment
Farming the ocean	Terrorists and terrorism
Genetic engineering	Unnatural food additives
Gun control	Water purity
Handicapped accessibility	Waste management
Health care equality	Wise use of land
Homelessness	World hunger
Human rights	World unity

Bobbie actively participated in the brainstorming session by raising questions and helping students identify their concerns in a concise way. She listened as they talked and worked with them to clarify and summarize their ideas. It's an impressive list of interesting topics, and it was generated by a classroom of fifth graders.

Although this formal method of selecting a topic works well for many teachers, some prefer a less formal approach. Rather than brainstorm a list of topics and then selecting from the list, some teachers prefer informal discussions. They like to involve students in an open discussion of the various topics that interest them. These teachers contribute to this active sharing of ideas with their students and guide their decisions about topics.

When students can't reach a consensus on a TI, there are other alternatives. As a matter of fact, this happened to Madge Sidwell, a departmentalized sixth-grade language arts teacher. When her students couldn't agree on a topic, they resolved the problem by initiating two different TIs at the same time. She reports that it worked beautifully; students in each group learned a great deal from their own group and the individual presentations of the other group.

Teacher-Selected Theme Immersions

All teachers have favorite topics. Sometimes they are an outgrowth of a hobby, such as rock hunting or bird watching, or of content they especially like, such as a particular area of history or political science. Occasionally the topic is something they loved to teach at another grade level. We know a teacher who had taught first grade. When she moved to a fourth-grade classroom, she didn't want to give up her study of dinosaurs, so every year her students have a dinosaur TI entitled "Why did they die?" The content is, of course, more sophisticated at the fourth-grade level. Students learn about the Ice Age, discuss the changing conditions on earth that caused the extinction of dinosaurs, and compare these with the conditions that endanger certain species today. The teacher enjoys the dinosaur unit, and it gives her a chance to unwind from and prepare for other themes that require more thinking and effort on her part. We wouldn't be surprised if she did an Elderhostel on dinosaurs during her retirement years.

Martha, a third-grade teacher whose roots are in the western states, does a TI on that region. Since she loves that part of the country and has taken numerous trips there, she has a large collection of materials, including photos, videos, slides, travel brochures, and children's books. Fortunately, too, regional geography is a part of the curriculum at her grade level. She especially enjoys sparking her students' interest in Yellowstone Park and increasing their knowledge about it. In addition to studying sites in the park, such as Old Faithful, she and her students also explore related questions: "How can tourists be kept from endangering the bears?" "What are the effects of automobile and bus fumes on plant and animal life?" and "What effect do geysers have on the environment?" When her students study the Black Hills of South Dakota, they become aware of the long-standing debate over whether Mount Rushmore is a beautiful sight or an assault on nature.

It's important to remember that student-generated topics some-times emerge when you least expect them. Karen Smith explained how this happened in her fifth- and sixth-grade classroom (Whole Language Umbrella Conference, 1992). She had planned to do a teacher-selected unit on survival and began the study by reading aloud a favorite book, Jean Craighead George's *Julie of the Wolves*. After she had read about twenty pages, one of her students asked about "marriage of conve-nience," and the group then discussed their surprise that Julie had married at the age of fourteen. As Karen continued to read the book, the students asked more and more questions and engaged in several lively discussions related to the story. By the time Karen had finished reading, she realized that she had to give up her intended theme on survival and get out of the way. Her students' interests led into a fascinating student-generated theme on comparative cultures.

Mandated Theme Immersions

In most school systems, certain required topics must be studied at each grade level. In our dream school, which we mentioned earlier, we would want to keep mandated topics at a minimum, but we realize that some schools do require that certain topics be studied. If you teach in a school that doesn't have numerous curriculum mandates, consider yourself fortunate and skim (or even skip) the next section.

What content are you told you must teach? If you teach where there are many mandates, it's important for you to know what you're expected to teach in a given year. Now wait, we aren't saying that you should teach everything, but you should find out what the dictates are. You don't want to be a slave to the curriculum guidelines and spend the entire year following the mandated curriculum, but neither do you want to commit professional suicide by not addressing the mandates.

To address the expectations of others, it's a good idea to study the district and state curriculum guides for all curriculum areas. As you do so, jot down the expected topics and note those you want to propose for study as well as those you think students are likely to suggest. You may be pleasantly surprised at some of the content that state legislators, well-meaning school board members, and others have included in the curriculum. In fact, some of the suggested topics may be of real interest to both you and your students.

As you consider both sets of topics, those suggested by others and those that you and your students select, we recommend that you look for commonalities among them and combine some of them in order to study fewer topics in greater depth. Karen Smith (Whole Language Umbrella Conference, 1992) considered the issue of district mandates. She felt a need to show some compliance with district mandates by addressing the topics in her textbooks. She studied the fifth-grade social studies book and noted that several chapters dealt with wars. Rather than plow through each chapter in sequence, she developed a study unit around the larger topic of conflict, and the class did a comparative study of wars. The students worked in small research groups, each studying a different war. Later in the unit, each small group shared its information with the whole group, which enabled everyone to compare and contrast the various wars. In this way, Karen "covered" the content of the book in a month and a half and did it in a meaningful and coherent way by finding commonalities between and among the chapters in the social studies textbook. Her students were then able to move on to explore topics that she and they developed together.

This notion of exploring broader topics rather than focusing on smaller, less meaningful ones finds support among individual educators and professional groups. The National Center for Improving Science Education, for example, emphasizes that students need to develop an in-depth understanding of selected topics. In their document, *Getting Started in Science: A Blueprint for Elementary School Science Education*, they state, ". . . if students are more intensely engaged in fewer topics, they are more likely to find meaning in what they are studying and will be better prepared for advanced study."

What materials are you supposed to use? In many schools and school districts, you are expected to use certain materials. When teachers look at these materials, they are often unprepared for the avalanche not only an adopted textbook in each area but often a variety of ancillary materials. Here again, we hope you aren't expected to use all of them. However, there may be some that really are useful, although you may not want to use them in the way the publishers suggest. Conversely, some might be nearly useless. One teacher we know uses her social studies books only for their maps (You're right! That's a lot of money to spend for twenty-six books when only the maps contribute to her program).

Due to the influence of professional organizations, teachers, and other professionals, the newer textbooks have improved. For example, new social studies books include primary sources, pictures, charts, diagrams, timelines, and maps that can be used as reference tools. Nevertheless, you probably don't need a copy for every student in your class.

What will your students be tested on? If you live in certain parts of the country, you know that an important concern of many administrators, boards of education, and the media is students' performance on standardized tests. We won't get on our bandwagon about standardized testing, but we do hope testing companies aren't dictating curriculum in your area. Although we'd like to tell you to have no part of it, we don't want you thrown into the lion's den. If you teach in a state or system intent on high test scores, it's often necessary to know the rules early in the game. The whole language teachers with whom we work and who use TIs have students who do well on tests in spite of the teachers' opposition to standardized testing. We believe their students do well because they do lots of reading, they write and publish often, and they are constantly engaged in research through which they continually expand their knowledge base.

Some teachers even have to document that they have taught certain key items on the test. If you teach where this notion prevails, do what some of the teachers we know do: make notes on the required information and, if you don't think it is that important, figure out how you can teach it in the most efficient and meaningful way.

What are some "must dos"? Each teacher must make decisions about satisfying the school and/or state requirements. If some of the "must dos" involve content that you think is unimportant, then spend only a minimum amount of time before moving on to what you do consider important. Some teachers incorporate a required topic in what they are studying and then document it in some way. For example, they use a bulletin board to display information on a topic for others to see. In this way, they "cover" the required topics but still have big chunks of time for student- and teacher-selected TIs.

At a recent conference, a speaker shared a story about a young teacher who was doing a theme immersion on space exploration, a topic that she and the students had selected. The students were excited about the theme, since many of their parents worked in the space industry. Everything was going beautifully until the supervisor visited, looked at the curriculum guide, and told her that she was supposed to be studying the grocery store. After the supervisor left, she told the students that they had to study the grocery store. Instead of spending three weeks on that topic, however, they spent one full day. When the supervisor visited again, he was impressed with how much the students knew about the grocery store and left satisfied that the curriculum was being "covered." The teacher and students then returned to their exciting exploration of space. Some might call this "giving a little in order to keep a lot." Other teachers find that they can teach some of the "must dos" as part of their themes. For example, if career education is a required area of study, they discuss careers that are available for people trained in different fields when it's relevant to their themes, so they don't need to spend time studying careers in isolation.

Teaching about famous men and women in science, literature, and other fields is required in many places, and it can help students further appreciate their contributions. An ideal time to have a Contributions of

Famous People TI is in the fall, when newspapers and magazines publish articles on the winners of the Nobel prizes. It's a great time to look up previous winners of the prizes and think about who would have been awarded a Nobel prize had these awards been made since the beginning of recorded history. One seventh-grade class had their own Nobel prize in literature and gave it to the Collier brothers for their contribution to children's historical fiction.

Some "must dos" may involve content or strategies that are in agreement with what you believe is important. Thinking skills, for example, are included in most curriculum guides. TI teachers constantly encourage students to think critically as they discuss topics, read texts, and engage in their own writing. Like thinking skills, study skills are usually included in textbooks and curriculum guides, and TI teachers emphasize these skills in their TIs by having students outline, summarize, and use graphic organizers.

What Are Some Sources for Topic Selection?

Earlier we listed several topics that a fifth-grade class thought would be interesting social issues for theme immersions. But there are many other sources teachers and students can refer to in searching out topics that intrigue them.

World Events

Almost every year, a world event, disaster, or human interest story grabs students' attention. Examples include the Gulf War over Kuwait, a major earthquake, a new discovery. In an area where a hurricane has occurred, there will probably be interest in hurricanes and other natural disasters. In our early years as teachers, the assassination of John Kennedy was a topic of intense interest to us. This tragic event was important in terms of our nation's history, but it evolved into a deep study of how the writers of the Constitution ensure order in the government following presidential assassinations and how presidential assassinations might be prevented in a democracy. When such events occur, the sensible thing may be to abandon projected work and follow the event at hand for as long as it's deemed important by the teacher and the students.

Local Events

Most communities sponsor local celebrations that provide a natural time to study a topic, and newspaper and television coverage often presents information that increases interest. The type of celebrations varies from community to community. We've seen teachers in Louisiana capitalize on their community's "Strawberry Festival" and teachers in the

Elba, New York, area put together a great theme immersion around their local "Onion Days" celebration.

The county or state fair or a homecoming celebration for a famous person from the region can also be a vehicle for catching students' interest and expanding their understanding. If something needs celebrating and the community hasn't caught on yet, a classroom or school could introduce a tradition. Students might get started by reading and talking about Byrd Baylor's *I'm in Charge of Celebrations*.

Local History

Some students, who couldn't care less about some aspects of the usual social studies curriculum, often become intrigued by the history of their own community. Fourth graders in Matt Chimera's class at Jefferson School in Kenmore, New York, became excited about the history of the nearby Erie Canal. It all started when they took a packet ride down the waterway. That trip inspired a study that led to many worthwhile learning experiences, including reading and discussing authentic diaries and letters written by canal passengers and workers and contemporary books about the canal dating from the 1830s.

Ethnographic studies of the community are real. An ethnographer, in the strictest sense, is a person trained as an anthropologist who describes cultures and groups of people. There are many different ways for students to be ethnographers and record their findings through written logs, photographic profiles, and video documentation.

Probably the most publicized and best example of students as ethnographers is the Foxfire project inspired and directed by Elliot Wigginton. His project at Rabun Gap, Georgia, has primarily involved the work of secondary students. The project has produced a number of volumes recording this important work and a foundation has been created that provides support for scholarships, buildings, and much more.

Foxfire is a good example of what can be done, and it has been replicated in many regions of the United States, mostly at the secondary level. However, elementary school students, beginning even in the primary grades, can also work as ethnographers, conducting research in the local area and sharing their findings in appropriate ways.

Researching a local community is a wonderful way to involve parents and community members. One excellent project we've seen is done yearly by Amanda Kutz, a graduate of our university, and a team of sixth-grade teachers at Laurel Bay School in Beaufort, South Carolina. The media specialist initiates the study with fifth graders before school dismisses for the summer. Students are given a pamphlet that lists historical sites in the area and they keep track of their summer excursions to these sites, for which they receive credit in sixth grade. We will discuss this TI in more detail in Chapter 8.

Family History

Another type of ethnographic study is family history. History may turn some students off, but their interest is usually enlivened when they dig into their own family's story. Family ethnography consists simply of students conducting research on their own family. They interview family members to collect family history and often make a genealogical record of the family, record family customs, and document geographic movement. The study might involve beginning a family archive to include copies of documents such as funeral and wedding announcements, deeds to property, old photographs, diaries, or religious records and books. Since most students engage in activities with their parents during vacation periods and often visit relatives in other areas of the state or region, a good time to begin a family history TI may be just before a holiday or vacation period. See Section D in the resource list (p. 183) for suggested interview questions and activities for recording and documenting family history.

Topic selection is perhaps the most important aspect of theme immersion. The topic must be something in which all members of the classroom community are willing to make an investment of time and energy. The central theme of study may be proposed by the teacher or the students, or it may be a topic mandated by the state, the district, or the school course of study. Regardless of the source of the topic, students, with guidance from the teacher, help determine the directions the study will take. We propose that students study a limited number of broad topics so that they will develop more depth of understanding. We suggest that social issues are of interest to students and, by studying these issues, students will acquire the knowledge and skills necessary for living in a changing world. We also recommend that teachers capitalize on children's interest in their family, in what's happening in the world at large, and in their local community to guide their selection of topics.

Implementing a
Theme Immersion

You have a topic for your TI. Now, what do you do? When we first started teaching, we thought everything had to be perfectly preplanned. Later, however, with a little experience under our belts, we learned that planning a theme is like painting with oil on a canvas: if you decide a rabbit should be a mouse, you cover up your ill-conceived bunny with a light neutral cover, let it dry, and you're ready to paint again. It's even easier to shift the direction of a theme. If you and your students find a better course, there is little that can't be changed.

Before planning, and throughout the process, a little song can play in your mind: "If they love what they're doing, if they're reading and writing, if they're discussing issues, and if they're really thinking, then I'm succeeding." During a theme immersion study of an environmental topic, for example, you might accept the unanimous decision of a group of students to stop studying how coral reefs are formed and start devouring everything on mangrove trees as they explore the importance of these trees to the southwestern coast of Florida. "If they love what they're doing" will play away as you see students using reference materials and recording their findings about mangrove trees. You know that, in addition to learning content and beginning to care more about their environment, their research skills are improving, and these will serve them well in future explorations.

What Areas of the Curriculum Are Taught Through a Theme Immersion?

Most, if not all, areas of the curriculum *can* be taught through a TI, but the nature of the topic, your teaching assignment, the school's organization, and your "trust" in the TI process will determine which actually are taught this way. We've seen entire curricula built around a theme, but we know this isn't a practical plan for most middle grades and middle schools. In a self-contained classroom, or in a team teaching situation and with a broad topic, it is possible to integrate curriculum around one theme for most of the day, but in a departmentalized situation, it is certainly more difficult.

The content of some topics is truly interdisciplinary in nature. Pollution of the environment, for example, touches on almost every discipline in some way. Community history, on the other hand, is more akin to social studies but will provide opportunities for study in other subject areas. However, it is perfectly acceptable to have an in-depth TI that is primarily science for three weeks followed by one that is focused on another discipline or one that is more interdisciplinary in nature.

As you move into TI teaching, you will decide how to relinquish control of certain aspects of the curriculum. As enthusiastic as we are about the TI process, and as confident as we are that students will learn and that interest in further learning will be generated, we know that you, your teaching situation, and the nature of each selected theme will determine the parameters of TIs in your classroom. You must be the one to decide that TIs can be your modus operandi for your social studies or science time or for a combined block, or if they will be taught in a truly interdisciplinary fashion.

How Long Does a Theme Immersion Last?

You can't predetermine just how long students' interest in a TI will soar or be maintained. Even the TI teachers we know say they often have difficulty predicting the intensity of student interest or judging exactly how long a particular TI will last. Most tell us that their TIs last for five or six weeks, but we've seen two-week TIs as well as TIs that extend over a much longer period. On a recent visit to Brisbane, Australia, for example, Maryann and Gary observed a team of two middle grade teachers implementing a year-long theme immersion on water that cut across all curriculum areas.

The number of available resources can make a difference in the length of a study. Some topics are captivating, but if you can find very little appropriate information, this, of course, limits the study. A primary teacher we know nurtured her students' interest in the Cahaba darter, a local fish on the endangered species list, but before long they had exhausted all the print and nonprint materials they could locate. She read newspaper articles to the students, but there was very little that they could read independently. A middle grade or middle school class wouldn't have the same problem because older students could read more difficult informational texts, such as encyclopedias, government documents, and other reference materials.

There are probably purists who think you should never stop a theme if there is still interest, but we know that in the real world of the classroom, there are times when you have to say, "Those of you who want to continue researching and reading books about whales can certainly do so, but we have to move into our next TI." In fact, it does happen that a class begins a new TI while some students stay involved with the previous one.

How much you feel you have to direct content makes a big difference in how much time you can spend on the TIs you and your students select. If your district has specific curriculum requirements and it is necessary to adhere to them, a careful review of these expectations may reveal ways to combine topics from social studies and science creatively and in this way to touch upon mandated content with some degree of integrity. You can meet requirements and still have time for the things students believe make a difference in their lives.

Getting Started

Students must be included in the development of a TI from the very beginning. This doesn't mean that you haven't given thought to the topic, but students must feel ownership early in the process. If you're repeating a TI from previous years, you will remember some of the experiences that were successful and some that were not. It's especially important not to rely too heavily on past years as you implement a TI because the prior knowledge and interests of this year's students will be different.

Making Lists

Our recommended first step for beginning a TI is very similar to one we followed when we first began teaching units way back in the sixties. As suggested by John Jarolimek (1967), a brilliant social studies scholar, we started each unit of study by making two lists: "What we know" and "What we want to know." We posted the lists for students to look at throughout the unit and revised them as our knowledge evolved and our curiosity changed. We still recommend this effective approach today.

As Connie Adams's fourth-grade class began a TI on oceanography, they made the following list during the first day's discussion:

What we know

- Fish, seaweed, sharks, germs, shrimp, lobsters, and algae live in water.
- There is salt water and fresh water.
- Water is fun to swim and boat in.
- Some water freezes.
- People travel on water.
- Water is used for transportation.
- Sharks sometimes kill people.
- Some animals that live in water have to have air to breathe.

After they had compiled the "known" list, the students gathered together for a few minutes in groups of three to think about what they wanted to know and to generate questions. Not all of the groups came up with questions, and students eliminated or combined those that were similar.

What we want to know

- Why is water cold in some places and hot in others?
- Why do some animals live on land and some in water?
- How do they farm shellfish in the ocean?
- Where did the rules about international waters come from?
- Why do people who drink salt water for a long time die?
- Why are tides sometimes low and sometimes high?
- Do people who fish for a living make much money?
- How can divers stay under water for so long?
- Why are cruise vacations so expensive?
- Is there really a Loch Ness monster?
- Why do some people escape from a country in boats?
- Do drugs come to the U.S. on boats or just planes?
- Do fisherman kill endangered fish in nets?

As these questions show, students display a lot of interest in content that isn't usually included in science or social studies textbooks. Connie was surprised by several of the questions, especially the one about international waters, but concluded that students asked about people escaping and drugs entering the country because of television and radio reports.

Now it was time for the students to propose subtopics. Connie asked them to look over all their questions to see if they could develop a list of subtopics that represented the questions. She reminded them that one question often relates to more than one subtopic. She asked them to make their own lists before sharing them with the others in their group. Before long, the groups were arguing about the wording of the subtopics, and Connie stepped in to help develop the list. Within a short time, she and her students came up with the following subtopics:

- Ocean tides
- Ocean depths and temperature
- Ocean animal life
- Ocean plant life
- Laws about the ocean
- Large bodies of water in the world
- Pollution of the ocean
- People who live and work on the ocean

When the list was completed, several of the students needed reassurance that all the topics reflected their questions. Connie also added an entry on underwater exploration because she found the subject interesting and thought students would too. She suggested that the group researching "people" include the cost of cruises question, that the "ocean plant group" research drinking salt water and farming issues, and that the "laws about the ocean" group study the killing of fish, drug enforcement, and escapes.

Webbing

After the students have generated a list of subtopics, we recommend another common practice: webbing. Some teachers begin the study planning with a web, and others use a web only after they have assessed students' prior knowledge and received their input. We could make a case for doing it either way.

Most teachers we know use the chalkboard for webbing, erasing as students change their minds and observe new relationships. We suggest copying the final web from the chalkboard onto a large piece of butcher or poster paper, so that the class can refer to it throughout the TI. (Asking pairs of students to do another web at the conclusion of the TI is an interesting exercise; they add many more categories because of their increased knowledge and interest.) Figure 3-1 shows the web developed by Connie and her class.

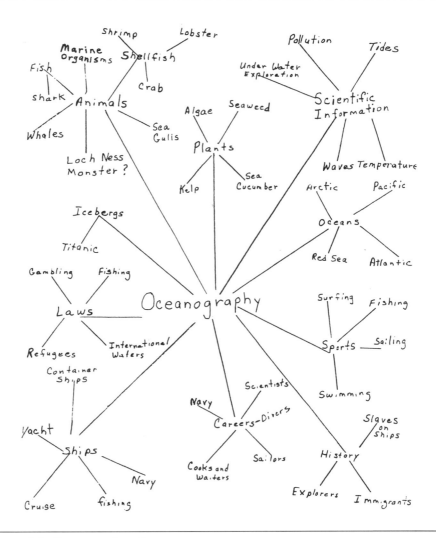

Figure 3-1: *Oceanography web*

Forming Study Committees

After completing a web or using some other means to identify initial subtopics, the students need to organize themselves. In Connie's class, once the web was on the board and areas of study had been decided she asked the students to think with whom and how they wanted to study. Did they want to work in a group with two or three others? What topics would they prefer to research? She asked them to list their preferences on the following form:

Name _____

I want to work with two or three others (circle one).   Two   Three

List six peers with whom you would like to work on this TI.

_____   _____

_____   _____

_____   _____

List four topics you would like to study.

_____   _____

_____   _____

When the students had filled out their preference sheets Connie noted their preferences. There were at least two students for each topic. Balancing their group choices was a bit more difficult, but she was able to group everyone with at least one classmate preference.

Brainstorming Questions

Children must be interested enough in a topic to raise questions and explore those questions through research. This is an essential feature of a TI. After the groups were formed, Connie asked students to get together to brainstorm questions about their topics. She also asked them to identify any issues they thought might be points of disagreement, explaining that more questions and issues would emerge as they explored their topic further. Each group recorded their questions on a blank transparency so they could share them with the rest of the class and hear their comments.

 When some wanted to refer to an encyclopedia, Connie reminded them that this was brainstorming and they didn't need to refer to other sources at this point. As the day was ending, she saw that the class would not have time for large group sharing, so she supplied each group with transparencies and markers and encouraged them to try to get their ideas down and not to worry about spelling or punctuation.

 The groups were ready the following morning. A few still wanted to read over what they had written earlier, but basically all eight groups were ready to report their ideas. The group studying people and the oceans presented the list shown in Figure 3-2.

 Connie noticed that some of the questions were unrelated to the topic but decided not to say anything at this point, thinking that perhaps someone in the group or another class member might point it out. Dorothy was the recorder for her group, and, after reading her

How many people work on the ocean?

What are the different jobs that these people do?

How long do they stay at sea?

How much education do you need for a job on the ocean?

Do different jobs need different skills like jobs on land?

How much do they get paid?

Is the work hard?

How many people work on one boat?

What is the longest distance any boat travels without going to land?

How do ships know where they are going?

How do ships have accidents and sink?

Do companies own ships or do people own ships?

What do ships cost?

FIGURE 3-2: *Questions from transparency*

committee's questions aloud to the class, she asked if anyone had questions to add. Several class members contributed their ideas, and Connie asked if the groups had had enough time to think of issues that might be controversial. Dorothy said they had, but did not put them on the transparency. "We think an issue might be about how safe the working conditions are, and another is if people get enough money, you know, fair pay for the work they do." Connie reminded Dorothy to write down these two issues and to consider adding the questions posed by their classmates to their list.

The teacher knew that most of the groups had more questions than they could research, but that this problem would be resolved as they focused on broader issues. The next part of the session was hers: a discussion on how to locate resources.

Identifying Sources of Information

Connie wrote column headings for the different types of resources on the chalkboard. The students were accustomed to this procedure because they did this at the beginning of each TI. The following are lists they generated.

Books and other print sources
- Encyclopedias
- Books about the oceans
- Maps
- Stories about sea life
- Cruise brochures from travel agencies

One student said they should ask the school librarian to recommend specific books. Others said they could talk to their community librarian. Ruel said he would see if the Government Printing Office had anything. He had found lots of information at the downtown federal building during the last TI. Amy said she thought the almanac might have answers to some of the questions.

Connie told the students that the science textbook had a chapter on ocean life and that they should also check the social studies book. She reminded them to share any information they found that was pertinent to the topic being studied by another group.

Resource people and media
- Videos and films from the library
- Computer network programs
- Home videos that people took on vacation
- Photographs from vacations
- People who had lived by or near the ocean, including those with summer homes

The students were concerned that they didn't know any specific resource people, but Connie reminded them that when they had studied Romania after the principal adopted a Romanian baby, they'd had the same concern. Later, however, they had found three people in the community who had lived in or visited Romania. She mentioned that if they found a resource person who didn't wish to speak to the entire class, they could interview him or her individually or in a small group and perhaps even videotape the interview.

Real objects and experiences

- Scuba-diving equipment
- Aquarium at zoo
- Science lab specimen
- Sea shells
- Dried fish at Oriental markets
- Big boats stored at people's homes
- Fish market
- Museum

Connie was pleased with the information the students had generated in the brainstorming session and began to think of some resources she could contribute. Researching the topics would occupy the class's efforts and time for the next couple of weeks.

Continuing a Theme Immersion

The groups are formed and students have started their research. Now what does the teacher do? Connie Adams describes herself as a facilitator and a guide:

> I'm in constant motion from group to group, individual to individual, guiding students as they find answers to their questions, helping them clarify their ideas, looking for books, and suggesting resource people. You name it, I do it when the students are engaged as researchers. When I note a problem or recognize an individual or group need, I issue an invitation to a demonstration lesson or maybe a guided practice session. For example, if I note that several students are struggling with outlines, I will announce a special meeting at the table at two o'clock. Of course, not everyone who needs help accepts the invitation, and some who already are outlining with ease may come.

Connie also whispers a special invitation to specific students she believes will profit from the session.

TI teachers know that reading aloud to their students is important, and many begin the day by reading a poem, a picture book, or something from the newspaper. In addition to this and a regular read-aloud time, they find other opportunities throughout the day to share a short piece. They read fiction and nonfiction, prose and poetry. They read whole books or excerpts from books, magazines and newspapers, articles, government documents, and other reference material related to the TI. They read for enjoyment, to model their own enthusiasm for learning, and to introduce their students to the variety of information sources. This infusion of content from the teacher not only inspires students, it also extends their knowledge base.

TI teachers are constantly on the lookout for information that will help students with their explorations of topics and questions. They also encourage their students to share any information they find that may be of help to other individual students or groups. When the teacher or a group of students finds a community resource person, other students may be invited to hear what the guest has to say even though it may not be directly related to what they are researching. Likewise, if anyone finds media that relate to one group's question, other students are often invited to view or listen to that particular film, video, or tape.

Progress Checks

Progress checks during a TI can take different forms. TI teachers conduct individual and group conferences, usually a three- to five-minute conference with every individual and group at least once a week. Many TI teachers also have students keep a learning log in which they record their thoughts and ideas about what they are studying; the teacher reads their entries at least once a week and writes a brief response.

Some TI teachers ask students, both individuals and groups, to complete a form at the end of each week to report their progress. Connie Adams uses the following form, which includes the information she deems important. If you adopt this particular idea, you may want to include additional items.

Name of Group or Student _____

We/I used the following sources this week:

__ Almanac	__ Magazines
__ Atlas	__ Microfiche
__ Audiotapes	__ Newspaper articles
__ Computer networking	__ Pamphlets
__ Directories	__ Reference books
__ Encyclopedias	__ Resource persons
__ Films	__ Surveys
__ Government documents	__ Textbooks
__ Interviews	__ Other (specify)

Three things I learned that I didn't know before this week are:

1.

2.

3.

I am having trouble finding information about _____

_____

Students' Attitudes and Achievement

Most classes include students with a wide range of attitudes and achievements. When you have students who don't get excited about pursuing their studies, you shouldn't necessarily blame yourself or, for that matter, the students. As Donald Graves (1983) reminds us, in a writing process class there may be three to five students out of a class of thirty who just don't seem to get deeply involved. We've all read books about classrooms or observed in model classrooms in which it seemed that all of the students were eagerly pursuing their learning tasks. In reality, however, they probably weren't. When your own students don't respond like the classroom of your dreams, you should of course analyze what might be done to improve the situation and not give up on certain students. But don't consider yourself a failure as a teacher because a few students may not become fully engaged as learners in your class. A number of other variables can affect students' attitudes and achievement. The following are some of the most common problems.

Some students never seem to complete anything. TI teachers have found that creating several deadlines for reports or projects instead of one big due date can help these students.

Another problem in TI research and reporting is the child who, even after demonstration lessons and guided practice, continues to copy her report directly from the resource materials. Dottie, a TI teacher, has told us an excellent way to avoid rote copying is to have the student report or write about what he has learned from a video, film, or other visual data source.

A few students can't or won't write. In these cases, it's important to ask for a small amount of written work in rough draft form. Students who haven't been in writing process classrooms may be afraid of being ridiculed because they can't write perfectly. When they learn that they won't be ridiculed or receive red marks on their papers, they will begin to take more risks in their writing. When they learn that you and the other students also make mistakes on rough drafts, they may relax and write more. Some students benefit from writing with a partner.

For some students it's very difficult to talk in front of the entire class. They may be shy or intimidated by earlier experiences and need to be supported as they learn that not all speaking situations are painful. When you have a rule of "no put-downs," these students often relax and are willing to present their ideas to their peers. If these students are responsible for only one part of a report, they will have an opportunity to gain some experience with oral presentations with the support of their group.

Group work often provides students with a support system that allows them to flourish, but a few either want to run the show or go it alone. Other students annoy their classmates by monopolizing the discussion and never valuing the opinion of anyone but themselves. These students need to learn to work with others as they engage in meaningful group activities. Self- and group evaluations are often effective in helping students improve their interpersonal skills.

Learning to work together in a community doesn't come easily to some students, especially those who have been in classrooms where they only engaged in and completed assignments given by the teacher. Helping students become autonomous learners who function successfully in groups is one of our most important aims as TI teachers.

Family Learning

It almost goes without saying that parents are important partners in a TI study. In fact, a TI is at its best when entire families are involved, including grandparents, siblings, cousins, and others who are significant to the child. In informing families of an upcoming TI, you might want to send a letter like this one home with your students:

> Dear Family,
>
> After careful deliberation, we have decided that the next theme immersion (TI) in our class will be on "The Sun, Moon, and Human Beings." Your child will begin bringing home charts that illustrate the amount of sun each day, the daily temperature, and the cycle of the moon. We will try to understand how the sun and moon affect the earth and how this affects people.
>
> You might wish to get involved in this TI along with your child by reading and saving newspaper clippings about such things as temperatures and tides. You might consider a family excursion to the planetarium during the next few weeks. Or you might want to drive to one of the hills surrounding our city on a night when the moon is full and try to identify the various celestial bodies in our solar system.
>
> You might also find it enjoyable to read stories together about various topics related to our theme immersion. Do you enjoy reading legends? As you find information and good stories related to this TI, please share them with our class. In fact, any ideas you have that will make the TI richer will be appreciated.
>
> Sincerely,

In addition to letters and other forms of communication, TI teachers get parents involved in a variety of ways. We remember how harried we were doing special projects or going on excursions until we discovered parent power. Binding special reports into books and other activities can

Natayla Clark reads a story about her grandmother to the class.

be simplified when another adult is in the classroom. Family members are also wonderful resources as speakers or consultants. Speakers don't need special credentials; some of the best are family members who have knowledge or experience related to a TI. Perhaps they have visited an area covered in a study or have read widely on the subject.

Family members also serve as partners on projects at home, doing a project with, not for, the child. Family fellowship and increased learning can result from these collaborations. During a family history TI in Sheila Patterson's classroom at Hayes Middle School, for example, students interviewed family members to learn more about their heritage. It's easy to imagine the strengthening of kinship between thirteen-year-old Natayla Clark and her grandmother as the grandmother told her story (see Figure 3-3).

Theme immersions enliven a class as students get involved in exploring issues that are important to them. In implementing a TI, teachers have to consider and coordinate a number of factors: the topic itself, the prior knowledge of the students, the amount of time devoted to the theme, developing good questions, organizing the groups, locating and using

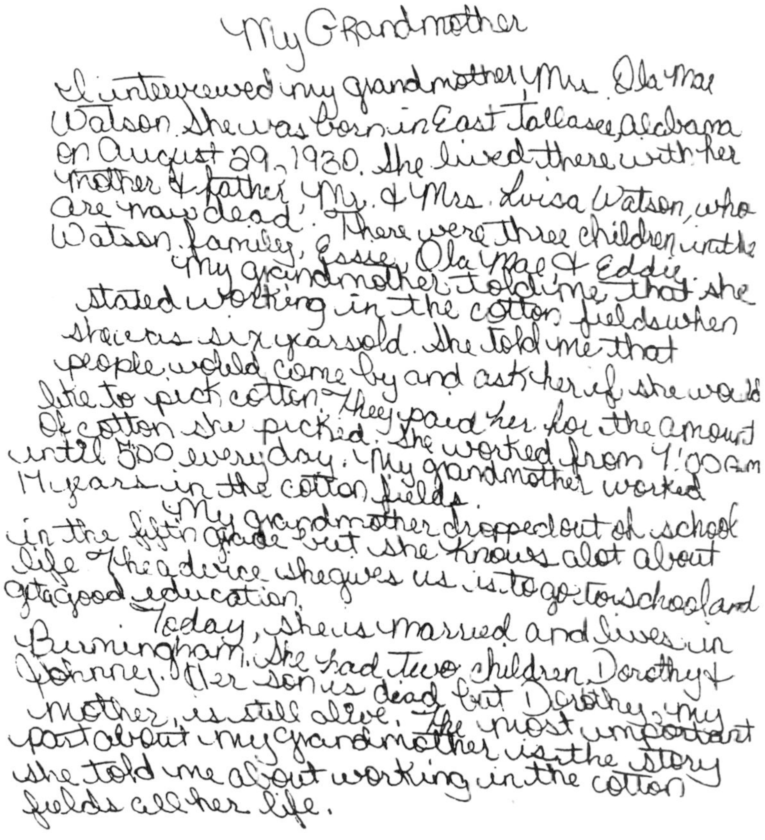

My Grandmother

I interviewed my grandmother, Mrs. Ola Mae Watson. She was born in East Tallasee Alabama on August 29, 1930. She lived there with her mother & father, Mr. & Mrs. Luisa Watson, who are now dead. There were three children in the Watson family, Jessie, Ola Mae & Eddie.

My grandmother told me that she started working in the cotton fields when she was six years old. She told me that people would come by and ask her if she wanted to pick cotton. They paid her for the amount of cotton she picked. She worked from 7:00 am until 5:00 every day. My grandmother worked 14 years in the cotton fields.

My grandmother dropped out of school in the fifth grade, but she knows alot about life. The advice she gives us is to go to school and get a good education.

Today, she is married and lives in Burningham. She had two children, Dorothy & Johnney. Her son is dead but Dorothy, my mother, is still alive. The most important part about my grandmother is the story she told me about working in the cotton fields all her life.

Figure 3-3: Natayla's interview with her grandmother

resources, and perhaps most important, nurturing independence in students' learning.

Getting started is never easy, and there is no one right way to proceed. As you consider implementing a TI, there are several steps you can take: (1) be convinced that TI teaching is theoretically sound; (2) read professional books and journals; and (3) connect with other teachers who have similar interests. There may be a whole language support group in your area and we encourage you to get involved. Armed with your professional knowledge and a network of professional friends, you will succeed. Years ago one of our mentors gave us sound advice when we decided to start an individualized reading program in our class. She said, "Plant thy feet in midair and proceed!"

Demonstrating Research Techniques

4

The title *researcher* should not be reserved only for college professors and scientists. Students, too, can be researchers if they have teachers who demonstrate for them what researchers do. Demonstration is not a new notion. We can think of several examples in the real world in which demonstration is a natural part of the learning process. Not long ago on a trip to Sweden we visited the Orrefors glass factory and watched glass blowing. It was fascinating to see the experienced glass blowers demonstrate their skills and to note the apprentices closely observing their mentors. After observing many demonstrations, the apprentices would engage as glass blowers, but always under the careful supervision of the expert. Through such demonstrations and thoughtful engagement guided by experts, novices advance step by methodical step to becoming expert glass blowers themselves.

TI teachers apply these same notions in their classrooms. You may recall John Dewey's idea that we learn by doing. He didn't mean only physical "doing," he meant intellectual "doing" as well. We cannot stress too strongly that as students engage or "do" something, they must be guided by a teacher who is an expert at "doing" it.

In this chapter, we show how Linda Maxwell, whom we will meet again in Chapter 7, develops in her students some of the research skills that are useful for exploring their questions and reporting their findings. Linda starts each school year with a TI she particularly enjoys. One of her favorite areas of study is that of the Native Americans of the southeastern region. She is very knowledgeable about this topic and has a large collection of experiences, stories, and resources to share with her students. She also knows that most fourth graders are interested in the

Linda Maxwell records information about Native American tribes.

topic, and that's important. At the same time, she meets one of the curriculum mandates in the fourth grade: a study of Native Americans in Alabama history.

To stimulate the interest of her students and to assess their prior knowledge and perceptions, Linda begins by reading aloud and discussing selected historical fiction and nonfiction books for children about Native Americans. She is aware that the children might have misconceptions and stereotypical images of Native Americans, and she tries to dispel these notions through the literature she selects. She cares that the students are exposed to positive images and knows that reading good literature is one way to develop a broader view. She doesn't avoid literature that has negative images but uses the books the children are reading to discuss point of view and to help her children recognize point of view. She wants her young researchers to think about the validity of their resources and to be aware of the different points of view held by authors and resource persons, so she reads aloud from a variety of sources on the same topic, emphasizing their differing perspectives. As students compare and contrast the different views, they begin to think critically.

It's important that children hone their ability to raise questions that will later help them to explore topics that intrigue them. To facilitate this development, Linda thinks aloud as she formulates questions so her students can "see" her thinking processes. Some of the questions she asked to begin this theme are "How did Native Americans affect the history of the Southeastern region?" and "What happened to the Native Americans in this region of the country that should or could have been different?"

As she explores these questions, Linda continues to demonstrate the thoughts and actions of a researcher. When she begins to look for information in an encyclopedia, for example, she says, "Which volumes should I choose? Should I look under tribes, Native Americans Indian nations, or Indians? I'll try each and see which one gives me the information I need." She pulls out the appropriate volume for each and skims the entries until she finds one that yields the information she wants. She doesn't assume that every child knows how to find appropriate sources for answers to their questions and she guides them as they work on their own and with their peers. For example, as students search for information in an encyclopedia or on a CD-ROM disk, Linda is there asking and answering questions to guide their research when necessary.

Let's look at another demonstration during this first TI study. Linda thinks aloud, "I wonder how many Native Americans live in the southeastern United States today? I could look in the encyclopedia, but that was published several years ago. I could call the Census Bureau in Washington, D.C., but that would take a long distance phone call and would cost money. Maybe we have the answer in our school. Perhaps I should look in the almanac."

Linda also demonstrates notetaking. One day when we were visiting in her classroom, she began by reading aloud a section of *The Dancing Drum* by Terri Cohlene. When she finished reading, she displayed a transparency made from the book. Using a suggestion in Routman (1991, pp. 281–284), she copied four paragraphs from the book on the left-hand side of the transparency and left the right-hand side blank.

The first paragraph of the story states that the Cherokees got their food from their farms. It lists what they grew as well as the wild fruits they collected. Linda talked as she made the following notes in the blank space to the right of the paragraph:

Notes :

  Foods : (provided by their farms)
(farms) Vegetables - peas, potatoes, cabbage, corn
(woods) wild fruits - grapes, berries, crabapples
(woods + streams) fish and game - buffalo, deer, birds, fish

Linda Maxwell demonstrates notetaking.

Linda continued to take notes in a similar fashion with the other three paragraphs. As soon as she finished the notetaking, she asked students in their small groups to select a page from one of their books and to take notes. Afterwards, each group briefly shared their notes with the other members of the class.

Through this experience, the students develop a clearer idea of what notetaking involves and can begin to use notetaking as they conduct their research. Linda continues to guide them and provides other demonstrations using selections from different types of texts.

Linda wants her fourth graders to be able to conduct interviews as a part of their TI research. Again, she demonstrates the process in an interesting manner by planning for an interview with a Native American. To broaden students' thinking and ensure that important questions are not overlooked, Linda puts some questions she wants to ask on the board, and the students add theirs to the list. To focus their inquiry during the interview, she and the students select the most important questions and put them on note cards. These are questions they chose:

- What was it like growing up on a reservation?
- How do you feel when you see children in school smoking peace pipes and doing war dances as part of a unit of study on Native Americans?
- What do you feel when you read that Christopher Columbus discovered a land with savages?
- If you could rewrite a textbook about Custer's last stand or any other such battle that involved overcoming Native Americans, what would you write?

Before the speaker visits the class, the students discuss other aspects of the interview. They decide to tape-record the interview if their guest doesn't object, so they can listen to the tape to make sure they didn't miss any important points. Then they are ready.

When their guest arrives, Linda introduces him to the class and begins the interview by asking a question. After she has asked a couple of questions, members of the class join in and their questions are interspersed with hers throughout the interview. In this way, students gain experience in how to conduct an interview. They learn interviewing procedures through an authentic encounter, not by going over these procedures simply to learn how to interview. Later, she and the students transcribe parts of the interview and talk about how to organize the information. The students are now ready to use the interview technique independently as another method of gathering information.

In addition to demonstrating interviewing techniques and getting students involved as interviewers, Linda tells students that researchers also gain information by writing letters to appropriate persons or agencies. She again demonstrates, this time by writing a letter to the Bureau of Indian Affairs in Washington, D.C., requesting information on southeastern Native Americans and relevant museums to visit. She writes a draft of the letter on the overhead, talking as she writes about the decisions she is making as a writer and taking care to show her students the revisions and corrections that are necessary for a completed product.

Linda also demonstrates other activities, such as outlining, that will help the children with their written reports. She develops a working outline on the overhead, and over a period of days, students see how she uses the outline to guide her research and report writing. At the same time they see how the outline changes in order to accommodate new directions in her research.

Using the outline as a guide, Linda writes her report, showing some sections on the overhead so that students see how she uses her outline

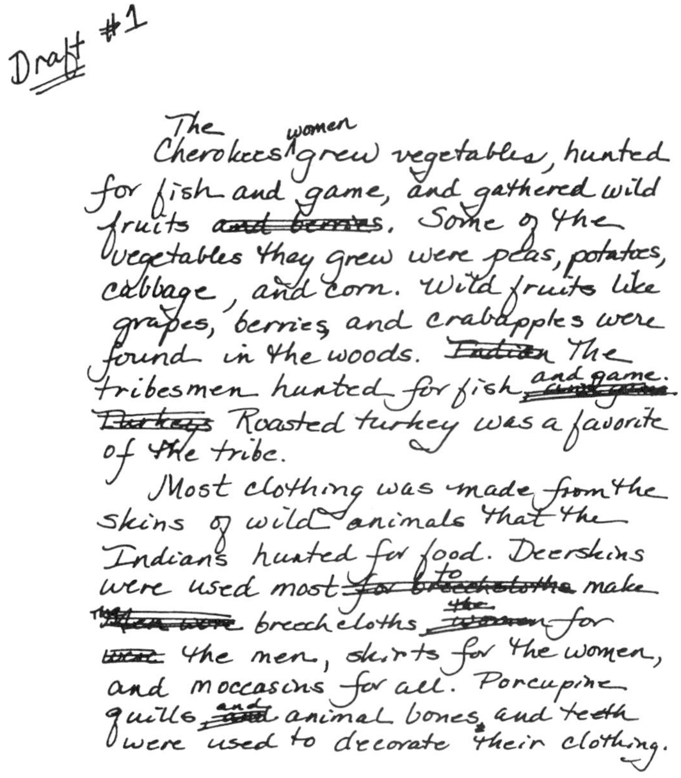

Draft #1

The Cherokees women grew vegetables, hunted for fish and game, and gathered wild fruits ~~and berries~~. Some of the vegetables they grew were peas, potatoes, cabbage, and corn. Wild fruits like grapes, berries and crabapples were found in the woods. ~~Indian~~ The tribesmen hunted for fish ~~and game~~. ~~Turkeys~~ Roasted turkey was a favorite of the tribe.

Most clothing was made from the skins of wild animals that the Indians hunted for food. Deerskins were used most to make breechcloths, for the men, skirts for the women, and moccasins for all. Porcupine quills and animal bones, and teeth were used to decorate their clothing.

FIGURE 4-1: *Draft 1 of Linda's report*

and her notes in making her drafts (see Figure 4-1). She thinks aloud as she writes, asking herself, for example, "Should I put in a little more about all the nations as I did in my outline or should I write a more in-depth section about only a few nations?" As the report takes shape over time, the students are fascinated by the journey and gain insight into developing and writing a report by observing an expert. Through such demonstrations and guided engagement, the students become more proficient at searching for information pertinent to their questions and at reporting their ideas in an organized and coherent way.

To develop their students' research skills, TI teachers demonstrate the skills they want them to learn. By reporting her own thinking processes as she developed a report, Linda Maxwell taught her students to

- validate resources by considering a piece's perspective
- use a variety of sources for collecting information
- take notes

Students share their progress on their reports with Linda Maxwell and class members.

- make an outline before beginning a report
- use an outline to draft a report

TI teachers don't make research assignments expecting their students to know how to collect and record information. They demonstrate the processes and guide their students until they are independent researchers.

Expressing Knowledge

5

Write a report! Give an oral presentation! Make a poster! This is what students in a traditional classroom typically hear from a teacher who wants them to demonstrate their knowledge and understanding of content. Now, there is nothing wrong with these activities; they are as nutritional to the mind as a slice of an orange is to the body. But why settle for a slice when we can have the whole orange? TI teachers want students to express their knowledge in a great number of ways and for different purposes. Why is this diversity important? Because it taps the creative powers of students who not only learn in different ways but need to express what they have learned in ways that reflect their emotional, intellectual, and imaginative powers. How teachers can unleash students' untapped capacity for expressing knowledge is the subject of this chapter.

Expression Through Replicating and Beyond

Replicating, that is, copying something someone else has created, has its place in a TI classroom. When students study Native Americans, for example, they often enjoy making a pottery replica or a sand painting. During a TI on pioneers, carding wool and making soap bring life to the study.

As students engage in replicating activities, they learn craft techniques and develop a sense of balance, rhythm, and contrast. Although there are many benefits to replication, TI teachers want their students to move beyond simple replication to expressing their growing knowledge in an original way. After students have embroidered a cloth using a

Students in Nancy Hagood's multi-aged class at Midfield Elementary School display a quilt that was completed during a TI on communication problems.

colonial design, for example, they might create their own design, explore the history of embroidery, or study and compare embroidery designs from different cultures and ethnic groups.

Most teachers are aware of the value of replicating activities as a form of expression and know that students enjoy and benefit from them. We will review several:

Appliqué. In appliqué, cutouts of cloth, paper, or some other material are formed into a design and fastened to a larger surface.

Basket Making. People have been making baskets since prehistoric times, and basketry is still a popular and useful craft practiced throughout the world today. Although supplies for basket making are available from most craft stores, students can fashion baskets from grasses, leaves, vines, or other plant materials gathered from nature. We recently visited a class in which students were studying basket making as part of a TI on Appalachian folklore. They explained "warp" and "weft" to us and recommended that we read *Baskets and Basket Makers in Southern Appalachia* by John Irwin.

Jane Butler's students finish a rain forest mural.

Beadwork. Beads are sewn onto another material for decoration, woven into material on a loom, or fastened together with string or wire. Beads can be made of wood, glass, or metal. Berries, popcorn, and other materials can also be used. An interesting study could be how beads have been and continue to be used in different cultures for money, trade, religious purposes, play, or decoration.

Carvings. Materials including soap, wood, and alabaster can be used to carve objects as part of a study and to give students an experience with a craft that began before recorded history.

Costumes. Making garments, ornaments, and other accessories from different historical periods and countries often makes a study more interesting and tells a lot about the people of those times and places and their changing way of life.

Designs. By making designs, students learn about unity, and they may also discover interesting aspects about different cultures. We still remember when we made copies of the hex signs of the Pennsylvania Dutch, which were placed on barns and other buildings as a superstitious protection against evil spirits, in elementary school.

Dyes. Dyeing cloth can be interesting and educational for students especially if they make the dyes from bark, berries, leaves, flowers, and roots of plants rather than use synthetic dyes. Many students love batik, an ancient art form with roots in Indonesia that is now popular in many parts of the world. Batik involves making a design on fabric, covering those sections not to be dyed with paraffin, and dipping the material into dye. The untreated sections of the cloth are dyed, thereby forming the intended designs.

Embroidery. Needlework in thread on fabric is a popular craft. Many cultures since prehistoric times have practiced a special style of embroidery.

By expressing their emerging knowledge through the replication of ancient crafts, students see further connections among the peoples of the world. Such connections are essential in TI classrooms. There is usually someone in every community who is an expert in at least one of these areas and these experts are often delighted to work with interested students.

Original Expression

There are, of course, many forms for original expression in TIs. No one form is better than any other, although one may be more appropriate for expressing particular information. A colorful mural, for example, will communicate more effectively the beauty of the plant and animal life in Australia's Great Barrier Reef than a dramatization. At the same time, a mural is not as effective as drama in communicating the emotions of the great Lincoln-Douglas debates. TI teachers encourage students to use a variety of forms of expression and to make appropriate matches between the expressive form they choose and the information they are trying to communicate. The following are some of the forms that are especially popular with our TI teacher friends and their students.

John David Oddo shares a representation of an early Roman house during a TI on ancient Rome.

Visual Arts

The visual arts provide forms of expression that include mosaics, paintings, and wall hangings. Those that TI teachers find especially appropriate are

> *Cartooning.* A cartoon picture, or several pictures with a caption, effectively communicates a message. Cartoons are entertaining while at the same time expressing views on people, conditions, or events (Benjamin Franklin used cartoons for such purposes). TI teachers begin cartooning by having students study cartoons in newspapers and magazines. We've seen some students make their own "Far Side" cartoons to express their ideas.

> *Illustrating.* Students usually enjoy sharing scenes showing people, places, and events. They can express themselves through drawing by using pen, pencil, chalk, charcoal, or crayon. They can draw on wood, clay, and foils as well as on paper. TI teachers often use children's picture books to show students some of the techniques professional artists use, such as block printing, scratchboard,

and collage, which can give students ideas for illustrating their own work.

Graphics. Many TI topics have facts and figures that can be graphed using bars, circles, lines, or pictures. Graphics allow students to communicate in a clear and visual way and to develop and understand the important skill of reading visual representations of information. Computer programs provide a variety of ways for students to share their ideas through graphics.

Murals. The creative use of tempera paint can transform a long roll of butcher paper into a wall decoration that also gives a lot of information on a particular topic. We've seen some terrific murals by students studying the ancient Egyptians and Romans, and prehistoric France. Students become especially enthralled with murals when they realize that people in ancient times used them to decorate their buildings and to reflect important aspects of their lives.

Photography. Photographs are a great way to share what students are learning. When preparing bound books, we like to Xerox photographs or use the computer scanner; this saves the original photographs for other uses and makes the book look more like a professionally published one.

Printing and Stenciling

Posters. Posters have been used for centuries to announce and advertise events. Students can print or stencil posters to announce special events, for example. We recently saw a student-made poster that promoted bottle and can recycling.

Scrapbooks. Like us, you probably keep scrapbooks of family pictures, announcements, and awards. Scrapbooks provide students with a way to collect and organize over a period of time clippings, postcards, photographs, and other items related to a particular TI. Students can print or stencil labels to describe the items included. Commercial scrapbooks can be expensive, but inexpensive ones can be made with paper, paper clasps, and a cardboard cover. A wallpaper sample book also makes a good scrapbook.

Three-Dimensional Art Forms

Students may choose to make sculptures to express their knowledge. They can sculpt the faces of famous people, or record a famous event in clay. Mobiles are also a good way to share information and at the same time learn about a fun-filled art form.

A *group in a* TI *on the solar system in Shirley* Lewis's *room displays their diorama.*

Construction Projects

Dioramas. Students can represent a scene by placing objects in front of a natural background. For example, they might paint a scene on the sides of a shoebox and place objects in the box.

Model Building. Students can represent buildings, volcancs, pyramids, temples, monuments, and natural wonders by constructing them according to a particular scale.

Movie Rolls. A succession of drawings or pictures on a continuous roll of paper is placed on rods in a cardboard box with a cutout front and the paper is rolled from beginning to end to simulate a movie, video, or television show. A written script that is read aloud as the "movie" is shown results in an interesting way to present information.

Time Lines. Time lines are especially helpful when students want to share a sequence of events or the contributions of people over a span of time. Time lines can simply relate the dates and information on a line but they can also include pictures or other graphics. We've seen time lines the length of a sheet of paper and others stretching across an entire room or down a long hallway.

Ginny Blackburn's students reenact a Civil War scene.

Diagram. A diagram is a good way to illustrate the relationships between and among different aspects of a whole. A diagram, for example, can show line and staff of an organization, subtopics under a main topic, or products and by-products.

Dramatization

Students love to communicate their thoughts and ideas through movement and voice. Some young children, for example, enjoy putting on a firefighter's hat and pretending they're fighting a fire. This dramatic play is informal and unrehearsed, and gives children an opportunity to communicate their thoughts and ideas in a developmentally appropriate way.

In addition to informal dramatic play, older students can engage in formal presentations, which they rehearse extensively and dramatize on a stage in front of an audience. Pantomimes, in which students act without words to communicate ideas, can enhance their understanding of a character or event.

Some students might enjoy sharing a story related to their theme by using reader's theater. Reader's theater differs from plays in that there are no costumes and elaborate sets, nor do students memorize their lines. The emphasis is on reading the lines of the script, focusing on the meaning of the text. As they read the script, readers use appropriate facial expressions and speak in a clear voice. Original scripts of many television shows are available and provide exciting material for reader's theater.

Puppets often enhance students' dramatizations. Students who might be too shy to act in front of a group often come alive when they can "hide" behind a puppet. Puppets can be made from sticks, sacks, cylinders, clothes hangers, socks, cups, and cloth. The stage can be formally constructed or made by simply draping a table. Puppets provide a wonderful avenue for children to communicate their thoughts in a way that is enjoyable for their audience.

Speaking

"Silence is golden" is no longer an accepted truth. In fact, we believe that social interaction is golden. Talking is essential in TI classrooms. Students talk throughout the day as they interact with one another in pairs, in small groups, and in the larger group, as they give oral reports and respond to one another's ideas.

In our view, younger children should not be expected to give formal speeches; however, upper-grade youngsters might want the experience of preparing and giving a formal speech during a TI. The class, with guidance from the teacher, would probably want to establish some guidelines, such as preparing thoroughly for the talk, speaking clearly, and limiting the time to less than ten minutes.

In addition to informal talking and formal speech making, there are other oral techniques such as choral reading. In choral reading, students read aloud either from their own copies of a work or from an overhead transparency. They bring a text alive by varying pitch, inflection, pace, and pauses. We walked into a class the other day and heard a group of third graders engaging in a choral reading of Byrd Baylor's *The Desert Is Theirs*. It was an enjoyable and interesting way to express their feelings about the desert as they engaged in a TI on the ecology of the desert.

Movement

In movement, students use their bodies to express their thoughts, feelings, and ideas. Movement is a good way to introduce children to informal drama; in fact, for us, movement and creative dramatics are closely related.

Music

Music is an excellent way for students to express feelings or thoughts about a particular aspect of a TI. For example, a subgroup on a space TI in Jeams Cowser's sixth-grade classroom brought in the record album

Debbie Horton helps students write a report during a health TI.

for the film 2001: A *Space Odyssey* and played it for the class. It created a feeling for outer space and set the stage for a grand class discussion.

Writing

Writing is a way of constructing knowledge. Students need to write not only to improve their writing but also to clarify their thinking. As students write, they must decide what to write about and how to organize their ideas. They may, as a result, see new relationships between ideas.

Students express themselves as writers in their journals, through research reports, and in written debates. They write plays, poetry, and fiction and nonfiction books. They write to pen pals both within and outside the school. Expression through writing takes countless forms. TI teachers have found the following alphabetized list especially helpful:

advertisements

advice columns

anecdotes

   from experience

   retold by others

announcements

applications

autobiographies

awards

ballads

beauty/health/nutrition tips

billboards

birth announcements

book jackets
booklets
books
bumper stickers

captions
  displays
  photos
  sculptures
cartoons
case studies
  local issues
  health issues
  historical issues
  national issues
  school issues
  scientific issues
  world issues
cereal boxes
commentaries
comparison shopping lists
complaints
conversations

definitions
demonstrations
descriptions
dialogues
diaries
  imaginary
  real
dictionaries
diets
directions
drama
  improvised notes
  scripts
dreams

editorials/letters to the editor
essays
explanations

fact books
fact sheets
fairy tales
fashion shows
forecasting
  future events

  future policies
  predictions
  prophecy
fortunes

gameboards
game rules
graffiti
grocery lists
guidebooks

historical "I was there scenes"
horoscopes

interviews
  real
  imaginary
invitations

jokes
journals
  real
  imaginary
jump rope jingles

labels
legends
letters
  apology
  commendation
  invitation
  support
  thank you
lexicons
lies
lists
love notes
lyrics

manuals
maps
marquee
math
  notes
  observations
  solutions
  story problems
memories
memos
menus

monograms
movies
mysteries
myths

newscasts
newspapers

obituaries
opinions

pamphlets
plays
poems
position statements
   ethical questions
   local, state, national issues
postcards
posters
proposals
   grants
   practical
   utopian
puppet shows
puzzles

questions

radio scripts
reader's theater
rebuttals
recipes
reports
requests
response to literature
resumés
reviews
   advertisements
   books
   documentaries
   movies

   outside reading
   plays
   songs
   television programs
rules

school newspaper stories
science
   logs
   notebooks
   notes
   observations
   reading summaries
secrets
signs
sketches
   of famous people
   of ideas
   of historical events
   of places
slide show scripts
songs
speeches
stories
   adventure
   fantasy
   historical fiction
   science fiction
summaries

technical reports
telegrams
television scripts
   commercials
   plays

wanted posters
weather reports
wishes
written debates

Technology

Now that teachers have access to computer software tools, which are available in abundance, their students can generate sophisticated presentations. Hyper-media, Hypercard for the Macintosh, and similar programs for MS-DOS are the newest developments in software technology. They allow students to produce excellent presentations by linking many different kinds of information—text, sound, graphics, video, and more—

Angela Hovater helps a student write a TI report on the computer.

in multiple combinations and layers. A new wave of teachers is beginning to use graphics, desktop publishing, speech synthesizers, digitizers, and networking to enable their students to engage in active constructivist learning.

Expressing the information and knowledge gained during a TI study through computer-enhanced activities gives an entirely new perspective to the importance of inquiry-based TIs. Linking learning with this important area of technology results in a powerful form of research.

In this chapter, we've described and listed a multitude of ways, from ancient arts to modern technology, that children can use to express and share their knowledge. Although we've suggested that copying a design is legitimate, we've encouraged original creations for one very important reason: when students can put something they know into more than one form of expression, they reinforce and deepen their knowledge of the subject. Furthermore, as teachers observe students expressing their knowledge in different ways, they are better able to evaluate students' thinking and to use this information to support further learning.

Assessment and Evaluation in Theme Immersions

6

When we taught traditional units, our major evaluation took place at the end of the unit. We gave traditional tests (usually on Friday) on the content that was taught, averaged these test grades with grades given on final products, such as written and oral reports, and then assigned a percentage or letter grade for the unit. Since that time, our beliefs about evaluation have changed dramatically. Although many TI teachers still have to give a grade, they use a variety of means to assess and evaluate students' work.

Assessment (the gathering of data) and evaluation (the analysis of data) don't just happen at the end of a TI; they take place continuously throughout the study. TI teachers use ongoing evaluation to guide students' learning, and they focus on what students can do rather than on what they cannot do. Although they value students' final products, they believe that what happens during the process of learning is more important. Rather than provide a comprehensive review, in this chapter, we will limit our discussion to assessment and evaluation of the theme immersion.

Anthony, Johnson, Mickelson, and Preece (1991) remind us of the importance of clarifying our beliefs about teaching and learning, since assessment and evaluation must be consistent with those beliefs. For example, if we believe that it is important for students to develop an ability to search for information, then that's what we teach and that's what we evaluate.

In TIs, students investigate questions that relate to a particular topic. With guidance from the teacher, they select questions to explore, locate and use a variety of resources, and report their findings. The teacher uses these activities in the assessment and evaluation of students during the TI. Assessment is based on the data gathered by students, teachers, and parents. Students accumulate their data in files and create portfolios of their best efforts. Teachers keep records of students' growth and development, and parents, too, contribute information about their children's learning.

Files and Portfolios

The student's file contains everything the student and the teacher want to save: drafts of reports, notes, summaries, outlines, logs, and journals. It is a repository of student work and expands as the year progresses. Students can reserve one section of their file for works in progress and another for completed, polished work. In addition to their own work, students might also include the group or individual reporting forms and checklists they complete during and after TIs. The items on such forms or checklists vary, but TI teachers have found some of the following ones helpful as students evaluate their own work. We include them, not as a checklist but as items to consider in developing a checklist. Upper-grade students could choose from a pool of items and create their own checklists for each TI.

Self-Evaluation During a TI

Item	yes	no	comments
I willingly read about my questions/topics.			
I read from a wide variety of reference materials.			
I take notes and summarize information when I read.			
I read newspapers and magazine articles that contain information on my questions/topics.			
I watch television programs on my questions/topics.			
I'm willing to change my mind if presented with new information.			
I try to be logical when I present my point of view.			
I ask other students questions about their presentations.			
I'm willing to talk with the teacher when I have a different point of view.			
I analyze my contributions to discussions.			
I'm improving as a presenter of my ideas to my group and in front of the class.			

Item	yes	no	comments

I share information in different ways, such as
  writing, speaking, singing, drama, or the visual
  arts.
I'm improving in my ability to write reports.
I don't worry about spelling and mechanics until
  I'm ready to publish my report.
I'm writing in different genres.
I evaluate my writing and ask others about ways to
  improve.
I'm growing in my ability to organize my research.
I'm becoming more self-confident in my research
  ability, in my writing, and in my speaking.

Gayle Morrison developed an evaluation form for her first graders, which they complete toward the end of their study. William's form records what he has learned about reptiles (see Figure 6-1). From

---

RESEARCH PROJECT EVALUATION

Name of Project _Reptiles_
Date _12-15-92_
Name of Researcher _William M_

1. Did you enjoy this research project? _Yes._

2. Why? _It's Fun to do and I like it._

3. Name at least three things that you learned. _Reptiles hach from eggs. Some Reptiles are born a live in dry hot dezert._

4. What would you like to research next? _Trees The ones that stay green all year._

FIGURE 6-1: *William's project evaluation*

it, Gayle sees that William is interested in studying trees that stay green all year long and can begin to look for resources for him.

Because TI teachers value social interaction as a necessary condition for learning, they emphasize group work in TIs. The following questions are helpful in getting students to evaluate their own participation in groups:

Item	yes	no
Am I an active participant?		
Do I respect the opinions of others?		
Do I listen to others?		
Am I improving on how I present my ideas to the group?		
Do I complete my responsibilities?		
Do I help others who are having difficulties?		
Am I kind and patient with other group members?		
Is my behavior appropriate?		

In addition to a file, each student has a TI portfolio. While the file contains everything the student and the teacher want saved, the portfolio contains work carefully selected by the student, which includes materials from the file. The organization of a portfolio varies; it can be organized chronologically according to topic, or type of material. Students include notes from their oral presentations and summaries of texts they have read as well as texts they have written. If done well, a portfolio increases students' self-confidence; they take pride in the work they place in a portfolio because it shows their progress and development. The portfolio also allows the teacher and the parents to evaluate students' work.

As undergraduates taking art classes, we kept our artwork in a portfolio. The art teacher guided us in looking at our paintings and drawings over a period of time and encouraged us to note the process and change in our work. Graves (1992) notes that artists have used portfolios for years, but educators have only recently begun to see their potential. For more information concerning the use of portfolios, we strongly recommend Graves and Sunstein's (1992) edited book, *Portfolio Portraits*.

Sonia Carrington, a fifth-grade teacher whose class is represented in Chapter 9, emphasizes the importance of TI portfolios and notes that a TI portfolio shows students' progress as researchers and as presenters. A review of the portfolio reveals how deeply involved a student is in a particular TI. Students include a number of different items in their TI portfolios—research reports, notes, presentations and projects, daily progress sheets, and self-evaluations. Sonia says, "Students who select items to be included in the portfolio and then reflect on their learning processes as they review their materials really begin to think of themselves as inquirers and learners."

To encourage this kind of reflection and development, TI teachers hold portfolio conferences with students several times during the year. During the conference they review the portfolio, asking questions and making comments to help students see evidence of their own growth as they reflect on their learning over time. Questions TI teachers have found especially helpful in these conferences include the following:

Why did you select this _____ for your portfolio?

How did you decide that this was good enough to go in your portfolio?

Who was the audience for this _____ ?

Why did you want to pursue this _____ (question, issue, topic)?

How do you think this _____ reflects your ability?

What steps did you go through in developing this _____ ?

If you had more time, what else would you do to this _____ ?

What did you learn that you can use in other projects like this one?

What did you learn about yourself as a _____ (writer, artist, actor)?

Did you make any mistakes that helped you learn something you can use in future projects?

Did you ask anyone in the class to make suggestions as you were working?

Is this _____ like the kind of work you normally do or did you take a risk and try something new?

What are some new goals you have for future projects?

Anecdotal Records

TI teachers evaluate their students continuously in an informal way. They make mental and written notes of their impressions as they observe students working in the classroom.

Many teachers keep a notebook with a section for each student. In this notebook they record information obtained from student logs, journals, presentations, and samples of student work. They also record their observations of students' products, make notes on the perspectives of parents and other teachers, and write comments reflecting the information they have gained in student and parent conferences.

In addition to their narrative comments, some TI teachers use an evaluation checklist based on what they think is important, including some of the following items:

Item	yes	no	comments
Displays intellectual curiosity			
Develops personal questions about topics			
Reads independently on topics			
Is developing in research skills			
Takes initiative in searching for information			
Takes notes			
Summarizes information			
Organizes information			
Is improving in ability to find information			
Displays increased vocabulary			
Looks for appropriate television programs and other media			
Uses available technology to search for information on topics			
Argues own point of view with other students and with teacher			
Respects other points of view			
Changes opinion in light of new information			
Seeks help from peers and teacher to find information			
Writes independently			
Revises texts			
Consults with peers in revising and editing			
Uses different forms of expression			
Responds to peers when they share work			
Spends time productively			
Evaluates own work			

You and your students will want to develop evaluation instruments appropriate for your TIs. In reviewing the sample items, please keep in mind a significant point Kenneth Goodman (1992, p. 110) makes about checklists: teachers often find checklists useful in evaluating, but whole language teachers are constantly modifying their lists and developing new ones. Many eventually don't use checklists at all because they realize they can evaluate just as well without them. We recommend that you involve your students in selecting criteria and developing procedures for evaluating TIs in your classroom.

Teacher Self-Evaluation

TI teachers engage in self-reflection and make adjustments in their teaching to accommodate the needs of their students and to increase their professional and personal growth:

Do my students know how much I enjoy learning?

Do I self-reflect as I interact with my students?

Am I extending my knowledge and use of technology so I can assist my students?

Am I growing in my ability to demonstrate research/thinking strategies?

Do I help students examine the logic they use in discussion?

Do I support students as they become risk takers?

Do I help students follow their own interests to answer their own questions?

Are my students aware of different points of view as they explore answers to their questions?

Do my students use multicultural resources?

Do my students read a variety of genres?

Do I use different types of grouping?

Am I growing in my ability to ask questions that help students make relationships between new information and their prior knowledge?

What About Parents and Theme Immersion Assessment and Evaluation?

In TIs, parents are involved in their children's progress. As parents confer with teachers, they provide valuable insights about their children, which enhance the assessment and evaluation of these students. Asking parents questions during a conference often encourages them to become more involved in their children's schooling and informs them of the teacher's expectations. Referring to the portfolio during a parent-teacher or parent-teacher-student conference is a good way to focus on the child's strengths and inform parents of the child's progress. Some of the following questions may be useful as you confer with parents:

How is your child benefiting from the questions he/she is researching?

What does your child tell you about the topic being studied?

What is your child particularly excited about learning?

What are some of the sources that are especially helpful for your child?

How does your child use the public library to find information?

What are some of the places your child visits in the community to find information on the topics being studied?

What television programs have been helpful to your child in studying topics at school?

What does your child enjoy reading at home?

What does your child seem to enjoy writing at home?

What are some of the topics your child has discussed with you at home?

What are some areas of growth in reading, writing, etc. that you've noticed?

What particularly pleases you about your child in relation to our topics of study?

How much help does your child require to complete the research?

Would you like to learn some ways to help your child become more independent?

What About Grading?

TI teachers agree with our views on assessment and evaluation and would like to eliminate grading, especially in the elementary school. However, many teachers are still expected to put a percentage or letter grade on a report card every six or nine weeks and required to use decontextualized instruments, such as standardized achievement tests and tests that accompany textbooks. If you are faced with this dilemma, you may have to give a little to keep a lot.

Debra Goodman (1992, p. 114), a middle-grade whole language teacher in Detroit, Michigan, who is required to give grades, explains how she meets this requirement. She uses a class list to record completed assignments and the quality of the work. She also asks students to document their work in a variety of ways, including logs and checklists. Toward the end of each marking period, Debra asks students to reflect on their learning and make a judgment about it. The students review their own self-evaluation and that of the teacher and then request the grade they feel they have earned. As Debra explains, she has to assign the final grade, but in most cases she agrees with the student's recommendation. As a part of her grading procedure in social studies, Debra asks students to complete the form in Figure 6-2.

Student Evaluation for Social Studies

Assignments:

Family History Presentation

Participation in Discussions

Family History Reflections

Classroom Study Project Progress

Committee Work

Other

In social studies, I should get a grade of _____ because:

FIGURE 6-2: *Student evaluation for social studies*

We agree entirely with Debra when she says the focus should be on evaluating learning rather than on grading. As Debra goes on to say, "I assert these beliefs by giving credit for learning invitations as well as assignments, and by keeping records of learning experiences as well as the products of those experiences. My gradebook accedes to the district demand for grades, but I have constructed it to provide information that is useful to me, my students, and their parents" (p. 115).

Other TI teachers face a similar dilemma. Madge Sidwell, a sixth-grade departmentalized language arts teacher, has to give students a letter grade in language arts every six weeks. Like Debra, she uses several assignments and projects to determine the language arts grade. In grading written research reports, for example, Madge uses the form in Figure 6-3.

Name: _____	Date: _____	Class Period:
Signs of Revision	10	_____
Appropriateness of Length	10	_____
Content	60	_____
Mechanics	20	_____
TOTAL	100	_____

FIGURE 6-3: *Form used to grade written research reports*

Social Studies Rubric

Category	Consistent	Inconsistent	Comments
Reads and understands a variety of texts			
Completes social studies folder			
Contributes thoughtful comments to group discussion			
Uses several texts to support statements			
Listens and responds to other students' ideas			
Completes social studies assignments and activities on time			
Completes social studies assignments and activites to the best of his/her ability			
Takes good care of all materials			

Final Grade _____

A—consistent for all areas (7 out of 8)
B—consistent for most areas (6 out of 8)
C—consistent for many areas (7 out of 10)
D—consistent for some areas (5 out of 8)
F—inconsistent for many areas (4 or less out of 8)

FIGURE 6-4: *Social studies rubric*

Ronda Vines, a fifth-grade TI teacher, also uses several sources of information to arrive at a grade for her students. She likes the suggestions about rubrics given by Regie Routman (1991, pp. 334–340) and has developed several rubrics, based on Routman's suggestions, for use in her own classroom. She uses the one in Figure 6-4 for social studies.

Ronda isn't really satisfied with her grading procedure, however, and is currently working to improve it. She is following Routman's advice about making grades more process-performance based than product based, and observations, interviews, and performance samples are also important aspects of her scoring system.

We've reviewed several aspects of evaluation in a theme immersion, including files and portfolios, anecdotal records, and teacher self-evaluation and discussed the grading issue that still confronts many TI teachers.

It's a struggle to move toward more meaningful evaluation, especially when many of us are still expected to administer traditional tests and assign a grade, but it is a struggle worth making. We are all continuing to seek ways to interpret students' efforts so that our means of assessment and evaluation are educationally sound enough to successfully challenge those currently being used.

Profiles of Theme Immersions

7

In this chapter, we give profiles of two theme immersions as told to us by the teachers. One is in Linda Maxwell's fourth-grade classroom at Edgewood Elementary School; the other is in Ann Stevens's eighth-grade science class at a parochial school in Birmingham. First, we look in on Linda's student-selected TI on the environment. We then visit Ann's eighth-grade classroom to hear about her TI on oceanography.

An Environmental Theme Immersion: Linda Maxwell's Fourth-Grade Class

Linda teaches fourth grade at Edgewood School in Homewood, Alabama, a middle-class suburb of Birmingham. The school is nestled among comfortable brick homes; Linda's room is upstairs and down a couple of halls. When you visit this classroom, you find busy students who invite you to join in their activities. They're full of enthusiasm and eager to tell you what they're learning.

Bookcases surround the entire room and every inch is covered with boxes of resource materials, completed student projects, and portfolios. (The students even have artist-size art portfolios.)

This TI teacher is constantly on the move working with individuals or with small groups. The students are in centers, sprawled out on the floor, and at tables. Linda usually carries a book or magazine that she wants to read to the students, materials to help students answer questions, or a notebook in which she makes anecdotal comments as a part of her assessment and evaluation system. If you see Linda or a student on the phone, they're probably calling someone to find an answer to a

WeeklyReader Teaching Master

What Kids Think About Presidential Goals

More than 40,000 students in grades three through six participated in the *Weekly Reader* Goals for the Next President Contest. Polled in mid-January, before the presidential primary season was in full swing, students were asked to choose 1 from among 12 key issues on which

they felt the next President should focus.

If you polled your students, they'll enjoy comparing their votes with the votes of students across the nation. If you didn't involve your students, perhaps you'll want to do so now.

Here's how students voted:
1. Clean up and protect the environment. (19.8%)
2. Help find a cure for AIDS. (14.6%)
3. Help the homeless find shelter. (14.3%)
4. Stop the sale and use of illegal drugs. (11.1%)
5. Work for peace around the world. (7.7%)
6. Reduce taxes. (6.0%)
7. Support equal rights for all Americans. (5.7%)
8. Help people out of work find jobs. (5.2%)
9. Make sure that all Americans have health care. (4.8%)
10. Fight crime. (4.6%)
11. Help improve schools. (3.6%)
12. Continue the U.S. exploration of space. (2.6%)

FIGURE 7-1: *Results of "Weekly Reader" survey*

question being researched, or making arrangements for a resource person to come to the class.

"Let me tell you about my favorite TI of this past school year, says Linda, "one we just completed on the environment. I have long had a deep interest in preserving our earth and consider myself an environmentalist, but the decision to study the environment as a TI topic was made by the students, and they really took charge. They accepted a lot of responsibility and pretty much determined the direction of the entire study.

"We had just completed a TI on Russia and needed to decide on the next topic. During our class discussion to brainstorm topics, Jason suggested that we look at the results of the *Weekly Reader* survey, which the class had participated in several months earlier. In the survey, they were to choose from among twelve goals one on which they felt the next president should focus. As a class, they had listed the goals in order of importance and posted the list. When we compared our list with the national results, we saw that the two were almost identical [see Figure 7-1].

Linda Maxwell shares information on the environment with her students.

"A very lively discussion ensued. We had rated 'clean up the environment' as the number one goal and it was first in the national survey. However, this did not make it an instant choice for the next TI. Students talked about each of the twelve issues and reported what they knew about each and why they thought it was important. They eventually narrowed their choices down to two possible topics, space and the environment.

"Before they voted, one child said, 'Why don't we study how to protect the environment here *and* in space?' The others liked the idea and the vote was unanimous: the environment was the new theme.

"The students started talking about human greed and how greed can affect the environment. One student recalled a quote from *Brother Eagle, Sister Sky* by Susan Jeffers that had created a lot of discussion earlier in the year: 'In our zeal to build and possess, we may lose all that we have.' He suggested that the class should keep this idea in mind during our TI.

"The students and I were excited about our topic. I immediately started thinking about what I needed to do to guide their work. Since I'm heavily involved in environmental concerns, I've collected boxes of books, articles, government documents, and newspaper clippings, all of which I keep in the classroom. We're also fortunate that we have a comprehensive media center with excellent resources on the environment. A lot of the students also use our city library, where they find more information. In addition, I'm an avid reader of *National Geographic*, and students catch my enthusiasm for the magazine and devour old issues. For this particular theme, the collection would be a rich storehouse of information.

"Before reviewing how we start a TI, I want to mention how we're able to implement TIs like this one on the environment in spite of the fact that I do have curriculum demands placed on me by the school district and the State Department of Education. For example, the school district expects teachers to 'cover' the topics in the adopted textbooks. In the fourth-grade social studies textbook, eight of the sixteen chapters deal with plains, rivers, mountains, and deserts. If we proceeded through the text in a traditional way, chapter by chapter, it would take about one-half of the school year. To save time, to meet the district mandates, and to make the content more meaningful for students, we developed a TI on the impact of the physical environment on people that lasted less than two months. In this way we covered the topics in the textbooks, which deal mainly with land forms, and went far beyond."

Getting Started

"On the day following our decision to study the environment," Linda continued, "the class broke up into small groups to brainstorm their thoughts about the environment. A recorder in each group wrote down their ideas, even if at the time they seemed silly or unrelated. I moved from group to group as students talked about the environment. When the brainstorming ended, the groups shared their lists and filled the board with their ideas. We eliminated those that seemed unrelated.

"Before we began our idea web, we discussed the need to look at the relationships between facts and opinions, and to think about social studies and science links to our theme. Following an excellent discussion and the development of a long list of ideas, two students went to the board and made a web. Since we had constructed webs, both as a group and individually, many times before, these students were good at webbing. Then Jennifer copied the web from the chalkboard onto a poster board so everyone could refer to it during the TI [see Figure 7-2].

"Six subtopics emerged from the discussion:

- Helping our city protect the environment
- Protecting the environment in space
- Saving the rain forests

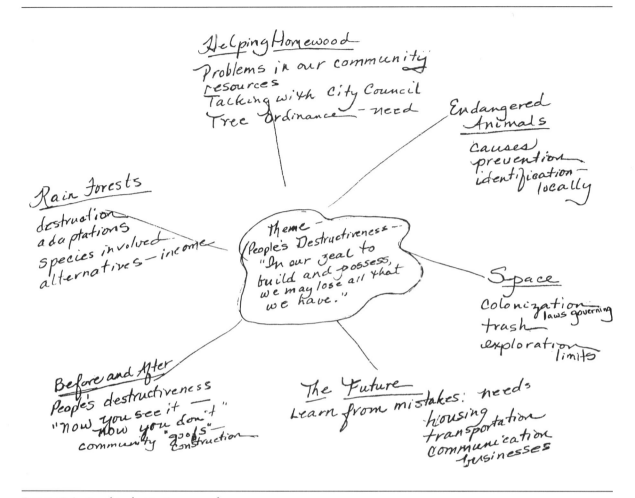

Helping Homewood
Problems in our community
resources
Tacking with City Council
Tree Ordinance — need

Endangered
Animals
Causes
prevention
identification —
locally

Rain forests
destruction
adaptations
species involved
alternatives — income

theme —
People's Destructiveness —
"In our zeal to
build and possess,
we may lose all that
we have."

Space
Colonization
laws governing
trash
exploration
limits

Before and After
People's destructiveness
"now you see it —
now you don't"
community "goofs"
construction

The Future
Learn from mistakes: needs
housing
transportation
communication
businesses

FIGURE 7-2: *People's destructiveness web*

- Our city before and after development
- Living in harmony with nature
- Endangered animals

"For this particular TI, I formed the groups for the six subtopics. Students listed, in rank order, three groups that interested them. All got their first or second choice.

"The students began working in their groups and formulated questions about their subtopics. The Endangered Animals Group, for example, generated the questions in Figure 7-3.

"After they had developed their questions, the committees shared their lists with the entire class. Members of the class asked additional questions, but I reminded the committees to choose only those research

What animals are considered endangered?

Where do the different endangered animals live?

Why are they about to become extinct?

What are some of the animals that live near us that are endangered?

What can be done to save the different animals that are endangered?

FIGURE 7-3: *Questions from the Endangered Animals Group*

questions in which they had a real interest. And off we went into our TI. By this point in the year students knew what to do and got started with little further direction from me.

"Since I value TIs, I made sure that students had plenty of time to explore their environmental concerns fully. The schedule for this particular TI, which lasted five weeks, was as follows:

Time	Monday	Tuesday	Wednesday	Thursday	Friday
8:00	opening	math	math	math	opening
8:15	math	math	art	library	math
8:45	math	music	art	math	math
9:15	reading/writing workshop ---
12:00	lunch ---
12:35	read aloud --
1:00	p.e.	theme	p.e.	p.e.	p.e.

1:30	theme	p.e.	p.e.	theme	theme
2:00	theme	theme	theme	theme	theme
3:00	dismissal	- -

"How we use the reading/writing workshop, which is scheduled for every morning throughout the year, depends on our focus and the TI. During this TI, we devoted our reading/writing workshop time to theme study. The students researched, read, and wrote around the environmental theme, and I conducted demonstrations and guided their research through individual and group conferences. In fact, the theme consumed most of the day. One day in math, the Rain Forest Group involved the entire class in figuring out the cost of a week-long class tour to the Amazon. They called International Expeditions and requested brochures on various tours."

Resources

"As I have said, I am an environmental enthusiast, and have a lot of materials of my own I make available to my students.

"In addition to all of these print and nonprint media resources, we rely heavily on human resources. My students got some of their most interesting information from people living in our community. One morning during our large group sharing time, we were all throwing out ideas about people who might be good resources on the environment. Jonathan excitedly said, 'I know a man who's saving Griffin Creek.' Later, Jonathan and I contacted the man, Tom Forsee, a scientist at our local university, and asked if he would speak to our class. Tom was a gold mine of information. He was very willing to work with us on the environmental theme and became a regular visitor to our classroom during the study.

"In addition to Tom, we invited several other guests to our classroom, and they, too, added a richness to our study. Jeff Underwood, a member of the city council, gave us valuable information about political issues and the environment. On one of his visits, a group shared their concerns about preserving trees in our city. He advised group members on how to get a city ordinance passed that would reflect their concerns. As a result of his encouragement, the Helping Our City Protect the Environment Committee decided to write a tree ordinance. After many drafts, and in consultation with Mr. Underwood, they produced the ordinance [shown in Figure 7-4].

"You can just imagine how excited the students and I were when Mr. Underwood asked us to present the ordinance to the city council. These fourth graders learned a valuable lesson. If they are politically involved they can make a difference in improving the environment. If

Tree Ordinance

For every tree cut down, there shall be one planted. If homeowners cut down a dead tree or damaged tree, they do not have to plant a tree in its place. However, if they cut down a tree that is not harming humans or the environment, they have to replace it somewhere else on their property.

If a developer clears land for a building, the exact number of ~~trees~~ cut down must be replanted after the complex is finished. A plan must be in the blueprint for replanting. If a developer fails to comply with this ordinance, his/her company will be fined the cost of the trees that were not replanted and the expense of planting them. Permission to remove the tree or trees must be obtained from a committee set up to preserve the environment in the city. The fine for not complying with the ordinance is $250.00 per tree.

FIGURE 7-4: Tree ordinance

The Tree Ordinance committee members proudly display their creation.

they write well, as they did with their tree ordinance, others pay attention to their proposals.

"The students continued to study the effects of development on our community. They examined pictures of business sites before and after construction. They wrote thank-you letters to businesses and developers that saved trees during construction and planted trees after the buildings were up." The letter in Figure 7-5 was written to a local business before the city council reviewed the tree ordinance."

Expressing Knowledge

"During the environmental theme immersion," Linda continued, "my students expressed their knowledge in different ways. There were many research reports in addition to diverse forms of written expression such as the tree ordinance and Planet Bill of Rights.

"I marvel at the artistic abilities of the students. The murals and construction projects were so creative. The toucans seemed ready to fly off the rain-forest mural. One group built a three-dimensional rain forest with before and after sides: one side complete with trees and tropical

A construction project made by the Rain Forest committee.

Dear Interlock, Inc.,

We appreciate how you plan to plant trees and put greenery beside our buildings. We are trying to pass a tree ordinance because some companies do not replace plants that are destroyed. You are helping our city save greenery.

Sincerely,
Sarah Johnson

FIGURE 7-5: *Letter to a local business*

Daily Group Progress Report

Date: 4/30/92

Group Name: Helping Our City

Group Members Present:

1. Foster 2. Crystal
3. Hans 4. Laura
5. Christie 6. _____

Today, we did the following:

Talked about ideas for helping Homewood such as going to Winn-Dixie and asking the manager if he would object if anyone would bring cloth bags. Discussed having a recycling bin at school. We arranged a date to announce Tree Ordinance on intercom.

Tomorrow, we plan to do the following:

Think of more ideas. Think of things to help restaurants recycle. Arrange dates for more things. Review what we need to do.

My group is having problems with the following:

Volunteers for the presentations on intercom. We need ideas on restaurants.

FIGURE 7-6: *Committee report 4/30/92*

forest animals and the other with a drab scene including earth moving equipment and modern buildings under construction. They made slides and transparencies for the media center and cloth grocery bags to give to senior citizens. There is no doubt that students learned a lot during this TI on the environment."

Group Progress Report

"I encourage my students to evaluate themselves. During this environmental TI, for example, groups completed a Group Progress Report every day [see Figures 7-6 and 7-7]. It helped the groups to reflect on their own daily progress and develop future plans. As I reviewed their comments, I could see their progress and note any problems they were having. By comparing their reports over a period of several days, I could fully appreciate their work. For example, when I compared the May 1 report by the Helping Our City committee with the group's April 30 comments, I

Daily Group Progress Report

Date: 5 / 1 / 92
Group Name: Helping our City
Group Members Present:
1. Foster   2. Crystal
3. Hans   4. Laura
5. Christie   6. _____

Today, we did the following:

We set up times for the ideas we thought up yesterday. We talked about grocery stores besides Winn-Dixie. We tried to think up ways for restaurants to recycle more. Saving cans and glass is all we can think of now.

Tomorrow, we plan to do the following:

Make a cloth grocery bag. Talk about pamplets that Christie found.

My group is having problems with the following:

We want Mrs. Maxwell to proof Tree Ordinance before we copy it. We still can't find restaurants.

FIGURE 7-7: *Committee report 5/1/92*

saw their continuing interest in cloth grocery bags. I also noted that they were still struggling with developing suggestions for improving recycling at restaurants."

It's Not Over When It's Finished

"If a TI has been successful, its effects never end. I want my students to develop higher level thinking skills and truly become inquirers. The environmental TI allowed students to pursue ideas and offer solutions for problems that were important to them, and it laid a foundation for approaching other problems. The inquiring minds of my students will allow them to set goals for the future that will make their lives, and the lives of others, safer and more fulfilling. I care about what students learn in a TI, since they will use that knowledge base for future learning. But what is more important, I want them to be sensitive to the global issues and problems confronting humankind and have the problem-solving abilities needed to meet the challenges that confront them now and in the future."

An Oceanography Theme Immersion: Ann Stevens's Eighth-Grade Science Class

Ann Stevens teaches seventh- and eighth-grade science in a parochial school in Birmingham.

When you visit her room, you know immediately that it's a lively place full of "sciencing" materials. Mobiles of sea life and stuffed tropical fish hang from the ceiling. Microscopes are available on a number of desks. The room is organized to accommodate the year's four major areas of study, with different areas of the room devoted to a particular theme. One wall is totally taken up by astronomy: photos of constellations, rolled-up star charts, star finders, star sketches, students' written observations about the stars on different nights, astrolabs, Air Force models and photos of NASA space shuttles. Nearby are cloud charts, a helium tank for weather balloon launches, and equipment for measuring different aspects of weather, such as wind speed. In another area of the room, a table provides a place for mineral identification, and there are bags of rocks and materials for performing different mineral tests. Near the mineral area is a large shell identification center, and there are models of different forms of sea life as well as sea specimens in formaldehyde.

The habitats, six large tanks, are kept along one wall and part of another. In another area of the room, there are aquariums filled with plants and animals. On shelves are orchid plants of all sizes. In a corner of the room, a child's large plastic wading pool holds turtles, which sit on rocks or slide into the water for a swim. From behind a tank, a large multicolored rabbit is as likely to hop over to its litter box as to a child's lap for stroking.

Amid this array of materials, animals, and plants, Ann moves about calmly in her white lab coat, conferring first with one student, then another. You hear her saying, "Are there any questions for me?" or, "You need to look at the potassium permanganate crystals over here."

Selecting Theme Immersions

Ann describes her approach to TIs. "Four areas of study—oceanography, astronomy, geology, and meteorology—are determined by the eighth-grade curriculum, and we're in touch with all of them throughout the year but focus on one area at a time for an in-depth study. Under

Students check the tropical tank to see if the conditions in the habitat are correct.

the umbrella of each major topic, students choose what aspect or aspects of the theme they want to research, and they do their research individually, in pairs, or in teams. I really encourage them to commit themselves to something that is of real and personal interest. It's rare that they have difficulty doing this, and the studies usually end with lots of experts."

Getting Started

"For the TI on oceanography," Ann continues, "the year begins with empty tanks just waiting for students to get busy setting up habitats. In fact, the eighth-grade students knew as seventh graders that they would be responsible for making decisions about what goes on in the tanks.

"The first week is organization time, in which both sections of the eighth grade meet together to decide what kinds of habitats they want. They begin by brainstorming what they know about oceanography and all the possible habitats. Through the process of webbing, they generate ideas for the contents of each of the habitats and then decide which ones they want to develop. Each year the habitats differ, as do the interests of the students. This past year the students created habitats for reptiles, amphibians, exotic tropicals, and marshes. All students sign up for the habitat they want to help develop. As soon as the list is complete, they set out to find what their animals will need so they can establish the right kind of cycle, such as the nitrogen cycle for salt water. Throughout the year, students can ask to change to another habitat by putting their request and their reasons in writing. If the request seems reasonable and it can be managed, they may change.

"As students determine what needs to be done, they make notes on a clipboard that hangs on each tank. This serves as a way for students to communicate with each other and their team members in the other section: at the same time, it provides me with a record of their observations and activities. They record feedings, births, deaths, and chemical tests on water quality showing such things as pH, nitrates, and oxygen levels. They record everything they observe. Whenever I note something unusual, such as algae growing, I look at the written observations to see if they have noted the same thing. If the pH is too high, for example, I will discuss with those responsible what might happen in the habitat if the problem is not corrected.

"The process of keeping the tanks going continues for about seven months before oceanography actually becomes the major focus of study in the class. By the time the full-blown TI begins, the students have a good background knowledge and their interest level is high. They know their research questions and many have already gathered a great deal of information."

Resources

"Our room contains a tremendous amount of print and nonprint media, much of which has been contributed by the students themselves. In one area, there is a big stack of Odyssey and National Geographic magazines and many reference books on science. There are several large files of newspaper and magazine articles on every area of science and a shelf of videos and audiotapes that really beckons to the students.

"I don't use the eighth-grade science textbook as 'the' text, but I do encourage students to refer to it as one possible source of information. I occasionally adapt study guides from the text.

"The students contact community members and agencies for information about their questions as they engage in research. These contacts often lead to intensive interviews and even to mentor relationships. Sometimes a student will invite a resource person to visit the class to give a lecture or seminar on a particular topic."

Becoming Scientists

"From the moment students walk into the classroom, they learn to do research like scientists. They write often and in a variety of discourses.

Students use many sources as they research information during a TI.

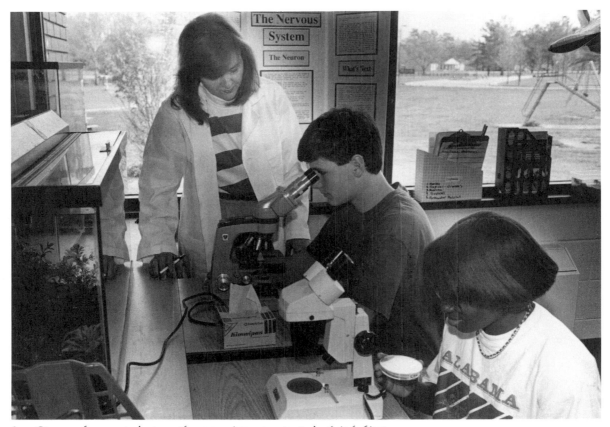

Ann Stevens observes students as they use microscopes to study their habitat.

They keep a weekly notebook in which they record their observations and thoughts about their work in science. They also maintain a file that includes detailed observations, copies of articles they collect, written reports they have compiled, artwork related to their studies, and bibliographies they develop from their research.

"They take notes when they read. [Figure 7-8 shows an example of one student's notes made as he read an article on sharks.] In addition

---

250 species (100 years ago)
Now there're 100 more
Great Whites are decreasing
Megamouth - new shark
Japanese raise and eat sharks
Steel mesh suits protect people from shark bites
Sharks don't get cancer

FIGURE 7-8: Notes on sharks

Object: test the presence of
Coliform bacteria.

Materials: petri dishes, pipet,
agar

Procedure: Make an agar
plate and pour water into
the plate and test what bacteria
are in it.

FIGURE 7-9: *Lab notes*

Habitat #5
The main test done is
the ph test. The ph is currently
6.8. We have cay, black mollies,
and red cap fish as well as small
goldfish living well. The fish eat
Tetra min Flake food which is
for tropical fish.
The water temperature is 59.6
degrees. The temperature is a
little cold and we need a heater.
There are three turtles that
live in the water. One of the
turtles, Simon, is currently
out of the habitat because she
has fungus in her eyes. The
turtles eat "Pepto min Turtle"
floating food sticks. Simon
sometimes eats worms and
bugs.
We need a new heat lamp,
but other than that the habitat
is stable, healthy, and growing.
During the third quarter, we plan
to add fish to the habitat, get
a heater, and add more plants.

FIGURE 7-10: *Habitat #5 report*

I am a scientist who specializes in new discoveries in ocean life. The next few pages are journal entries from my visit to the Galapagos rift. The Galapagos rift is a large vent on the ocean floor. These vents warm the ocean floor, thus, producing an oasis of life.

Day 1
I arrived on the small island where my small research crew and I were to set up camp. We unloaded box after box of sonar equipment. Then finally at around 3:00 my crew and I unloaded the heart and lungs of our exhibition—our submersible. We loaded our equipment into the submersible and prepared our dive.

Day 2
I awoke bright and early. I commenced on preparing for our dive by loading up any last minute things. My crew joined me and we dove. We peered around in the deep abyss for several hours, but there was no sign of any vents. We saw one lonely sting ray but that was it. No one really said much at dinner. We couldn't believe we didn't see a thing. Well, maybe tomorrow.
Day 3 . . .

FIGURE 7-11: *Fictional narrative*

to taking notes on what they read, students keep lab notes, which entail a different kind of writing." Figure 7-9 shows one student's lab notes.

Expressing Knowledge

"Students express their knowledge in a number of different ways. I strongly emphasize writing in all my science classes, and you will see students engaged in different types of writing. One student wrote a report [shown in Figure 7-10] shortly after the habitat was established In addition to observational notes, students write fictional narratives." In the narrative shown in Figure 7-11, a student pretends he is on Galapagos rift. He continued the story for several more days and told what he discovered and did in the Galapagos rift. "By reading what students write," Ann continued, "I become so much more aware of what they're learning. This is especially true when they incorporate factual knowledge into their fictional accounts. I feel more confident that the knowledge is theirs and will remain with them long after they've left eighth grade.

"We are fortunate that there is tremendous cooperation among all the seventh- and eighth-grade teachers in our school. When students are working on projects, the teachers can sometimes get together during

Students show their sea life made of papier-mâché.

the school day to plan how to coordinate experiences in the dif-ferent content areas. The art and music teachers are also helpful in finding natural connections between their programs and the TIs. One day, to my surprise, the students brought in delicate stuffed fish they had made in art class. On another day, the small school band played a song of celebration at the launching of our weather balloons.

"And I must brag about the students. Because my students are such active scientists, they have won several science olympiads and other contests in the region. And they're so grown-up and self-directed. They keep up with all the finances for the different projects. They ask for contributions from parents and find sponsors for our pet store pur-chases. Without prodding, they write thank-you notes and remember those who helped us during the year."

Reflections on the Theme Immersion Profiles

These two theme immersions embody much of what TI teaching is about. Both TIs focused on broad issues that allowed the study of many related subtopics of interest to students; Ann's TI was curriculum man-dated, but much of its content and direction was determined by the students rather than predetermined by the teacher or the school. Relevant reading and writing activities permeated both TIs. Students practiced literacy skills as they engaged in meaningful pursuits related to their themes. Classroom activities were authentic, real-world pursuits. And in both TIs there were many opportunities for student interaction and collaboration. They had choices and their interests were valued.

Interviews with
Theme Immersion Teachers

8

During the past year, we've worked with several outstanding TI teachers. Stepping into their classrooms enlivens our spirits. We interviewed these teachers and, in this chapter, give highlights from the interviews so that you can vicariously enter their classrooms and experience the tone and quality of the learning that occurs.

Gayle Morrison talks about how she guides her first graders in becoming researchers. Ginny Hart, a second-grade teacher, tells about moving from theme units to theme immersion and how books nurture the intellectual growth of her students. Phillip Westbrook explains how he turns a mandated third-grade study of communities into an exciting TI. At the fourth-grade level, four teachers (Ginny Blackburn, Jody Brewer, Ann Dominick, and Sherry Parrish) reveal the benefits of cooperatively planning and implementing a TI. Naomi Goss, a fifth-grade teacher, gives insights about how she raises the social consciousness of her students. Amanda Kutz tells how she and the teachers in her sixth-grade departmentalized team implemented a TI on local history. In the last interview, Debra Rust describes the B.A.T. Club, which was an outgrowth of a TI on saving the earth. (Note: The questions in italic are asked by the interviewers, Roberta, Gary, and Maryann.)

First Grade: Gayle Morrison

Gayle, a first-grade teacher at Woodrow Wilson School, has been using TIs for several years. Her inner-city first graders all read and write, and they develop into active researchers. As the first president of the

Gayle Morrison helps a group of students collect information.

Birmingham area TAWL (Teachers Applying Whole Language), Gayle's a whole language leader in our area.

We've seen your first grade students engaging in research projects. How do you get first graders started as researchers?

GAYLE: I do wait until October to begin. I then form research groups with four kids in each group, and they choose what they want to research. In the beginning, I demonstrate the steps of research, and then we go through the steps together. After I demonstrate note-taking, they make notes from tapes, magazines, and books.

How can they do research if they can't read the resource material?

GAYLE: There are lots of ways in my room. I have many of the Troll I *Can Read* series and other easy books. I read countless books to my class and I read aloud several times a day to students who bring books to me. I encourage them to get into pairs and help each other read. You'd be surprised how they can figure out meaning if they really want to know about the topic. I also put books and articles on tape so they can listen to them. Some of the older students in the school make tapes for me. I now have an extensive library of tapes about different topics. My students find so many articles that they want to read from *Zoo Book*, *Your Backyard*, *Ranger Rick*, and *Highlights for Children*, but in the beginning someone must read to them.

We know they take notes before they're writing very much. Tell us how this happens.

GAYLE: In each group, one child is the secretary and makes a list of all ideas. After a while, other members can take notes if they want to. I enjoy reading their invented spelling, and I think it's wonderful how they represent their ideas in such a logical manner.

How do they go about writing their reports?

GAYLE: When they've finished taking notes, they discuss what they want in their reports. After they've agreed about what they want, they use their notes and draft their report. I then write the report on the computer (they do this themselves later in the year), and the group illustrates it.

How are TI topics decided?

GAYLE: Almost all of the topics come from the interests of the kids. Because we have pet amphibians and reptiles in the room, that's what they usually want to research first. The fourth-grade teacher, Mrs. Vines, is also a TI teacher, and her students give oral reports on their topics of study to my students. Often when they share with us about what they're doing, mine want to learn more about that also. When the fourth graders gave reports to us on the contributions of owls to the life cycle in our area, it wasn't long before my students wanted to study owls. Articles in magazines such as *Weekly Reader* and *National Geographic World* spark interests that sometimes become TIs, and, of course, sometimes I suggest a TI topic.

Your room is packed with books and print of all kinds. We know you didn't get it all from the Board of Education. Tell us about your collection.

GAYLE: Yes, I have a big collection and I add about five hundred books a year to my room; I now have over five thousand. and I'm running out of room even though I keep buying new bookcases. I go to lots of professional conferences where I buy some books, but that gets expensive. Almost all of my books come from thrift stores and garage sales. Just about every Saturday morning I make the rounds of the stores and sales.

How do you stay current in your educational practices?

GAYLE: I read all the time; I spend a lot of money on professional books. And I read journals such as *The Reading Teacher*, *Language Arts*, and *Teaching K–8*. I attend the annual conference of IRA (International

Gayle Morrison's students select books from her extensive classroom library.

Reading Association) and Whole Language Umbrella in addition to our local and state groups. Through these meetings, I connect with other highly dedicated and professional teachers in our area, state, and country. For example, I've learned so much from professional teachers like Kittye Copeland from Missouri, and Wendy Hood of Tucson. I love learning and I hope I keep growing as a learner and teacher.

Second Grade: Ginny Hart

Ginny, a second-grade teacher at Hall Kent School, has been a whole language teacher for many years, but says she's only now becoming a TI teacher. Always a learner, she constantly engages in self-reflection, reads professional literature, interacts with other professionals, and is a real "kid watcher."

Why did you decide to become a TI teacher?

GINNY: I've organized content around themes since I first started teach-ing, but somehow I always had the uncomfortable feeling that something was missing. I'm not sure I can tell you what was wrong, but I do know there was too much teacher direction and that I was

Ginny Hart explores volcanoes with her students.

using too much energy and time on peripheral kinds of things. Instead of focusing enough on the learners, I was always running around getting materials or making something to put in a center. I knew children should have options in the classroom so I would decide what I thought they should learn and give them options, but the options were limited and created by me. Anyway, I am trying to move away from that model and I did a fairly good job last year. I got lots of good advice from Joy Tate, supervisor of primary curriculum at Karori West School in Wellington, New Zealand, when she was in Birmingham and when I visited her school in New Zealand. Kittye Copeland of Columbia, Missouri, was also a big help. In fact, I regularly correspond with both of them and they continue to offer support and guidance. They're so willing to respond to my questions and concerns.

Tell us about some of the changes you've made.

GINNY: First, and most important, I now use genre studies, and much of my curriculum emerges from the books. I have always had a literature-based program—that is, I read aloud, used trade books as the core of literacy instruction, and brought in every book I could find related to our themes. The children could choose what books to read, but I almost always decided how they should extend the texts. Now that we emphasize genre study for language arts—that is, we focus on one type of literature at a time—things are better. I have taken myself out of the role of chief decision maker, the children are much more involved, and topics for individual, group, or whole class extensions and research just emerge naturally. Of course, every book or genre doesn't lead to a class TI.

Could you give us examples of how some of your genre studies lead to TIs?

GINNY: During our genre study of historical fiction, the book I read aloud was Laura Ingalls Wilder's *Little House in the Big Woods*. There were so many questions about Laura's life and what life was like in early America that we did a class TI on pioneers. Most of the students really liked historical fiction and, in addition to our pioneer TI, a few students did individual projects as a result of books they were reading. This is how it began, individual students taking responsibility for deciding what they wanted to do with a text, but it wasn't easy. Some took responsibility, others didn't.

How did you solve that problem?

GINNY: It isn't solved, but more responded during our genre study of fairy tales. I used fairy tales for small group guided reading and asked them what they wanted to do to extend the text. Some took the responsibility, and again, others did not. The whole group talked about fairy tales and about what you could do with a fairy tale. We talked about the times when fairy tales were told and written down and about castles and knights. We talked about the reasons for fairy tales and compared different versions of the same tale. I wanted them to choose *something* they really wanted to do and that would be of interest to them. One student chose knights, what they wore and the different kinds of knights. Another turned a fairy tale into a play. Several chose to work together to build a castle. I felt better during this study—students *themselves* were beginning to decide what to do with a text. Teaching them to accept this responsibility is very important, but I knew it was only a first step. What I needed to do now was to help them develop their research skills and to extend content across more curriculum areas.

Did you do this through genre study, too?

GINNY: Yes, but first I had to teach them how to take notes. Regie Routman's (1991) suggestions in *Invitations* were a great help here. I put a text on the overhead and we made notes together about things they wanted to remember. They then practiced notetaking in

A student in Ginny Hart's room records his knowledge about tunnels after reading a Gail Gibbon book.

pairs by using articles selected from children's magazines. *Ranger Rick*, *National Geographic World*, *Big Back Yard*, and *3-2-1 Contact* provided excellent practice material and led into a genre study of nonfiction science-related books. They were beginning to be real notetakers and I was thrilled with their work. Relying upon their notes, one group did a mind map about the life cycle of butterflies, and another group wrote a riddle book using factual information about insects and animals. Still another group researched predators, and their report included specifics on how predators got their name, what they ate and what or who were the predators' enemies.

And this expository study led to an author study of Gail Gibbons and her work and spawned some new TIs?

GINNY: Indirectly, yes. During this genre study, I was reading a Gail Gibbons book daily. As you know, her books are wonderful examples of expository writing and she's written so many of them. I wasn't sure which of her books would best spark a special interest but happily I selected *Up Goes the Skyscraper* and *How a House Is Built*. A new basketball court was being built at our school at this time, and before I knew it, several kids were writing a book describing the construction of the basketball court. They were emulating Gail Gibbons's style! This led to a TI on building things, or what we later called our architecture TI. They learned about our original school building, each addition, and the ten-year plan for remodeling. The building supervisor, Mr. Lawley, brought blueprints of the school and a book on how to read blueprint symbols. He took them on a tour of the school and taught them how to read blueprints. Before long they had studied the structural plans, the plumbing plans, and the mechanical and electrical plans and decided to design a new addition to the school. One group looked at the history of school buildings in America. They made connections between this TI and our study of pioneers as they compared today's schools with the one-room schoolhouses on the prairie. I won't go into more detail, but I hope future students will decide on an architecture TI because, like any really good theme immersion, it touches upon so many different areas of knowledge—history, literature, sociology, mathematics, and geography, to name but a few. I loved it and learned lots myself. It's exciting to follow the interests of the children.

Sounds like TIs are alive and well in your room.

GINNY: Yes, we're constantly engaged in TIs—that is, inquiry, children's choices, reading and writing across the curriculum, and literature study as individuals, in small groups, and with the whole class. Come visit and you will see several TIs in progress at the same time. I simply won't make a child or group stop researching if they're truly absorbed in a topic.

I told you in the beginning of this interview that I was *in process* and I've tried to capture some of the things that happened last year. I can't tell you what I'll do next year because I will grow and change and I'll have a different group of children. I was really thrilled, though, when Joy Tate returned to Birmingham last year and during a visit to my classroom said, "I feel as if I'm in my school in New Zealand." If you've visited classrooms in New Zealand, you know what that meant to me.

Third Grade: Phillip Westbrook

Phillip, a third-grade teacher at Shades Cahaba, is very active in our area's constructivist math group. When you enter his classroom, you sense his respect for the thinking of his students as he asks questions and encourages social interaction. There's always an exciting TI in progress.

Phillip Westbrook shows a picture of an early Homewood house.

Will you tell us about a TI that you especially like?

PHILLIP: That's difficult because I like all of them. With some, my enthusiasm grows as we get into the topic, while with others I was
interested from the beginning. Let me discuss a mandated TI on
communities that I like. I don't like to have one set time block for
this as it can be a part of so many activities and experiences
throughout the year. This past year, the students had really built a
lot of background knowledge before the actual TI.

How did this happen?

PHILLIP: I called attention to the community whenever it seemed appropriate. When I read a book to them or had an individual book
conference, we talked about the setting and how people's lives are
affected because of the time and place in which they live. We
walked around the school community a lot and found all kinds of
excuses to get into the broader community. When we walked to the
public library for our research, we took different routes and talked
about the area, about why the planners and builders may have
chosen a particular site for a house or building. We especially

Students write a report on model communities.

noted the public buildings, such as the fire station and city hall. Our community is small, so we sometimes stopped at city hall and chatted with the mayor or a member of the city council.

So you built background knowledge about communities at every opportunity. Did you have a formal or regular TI on communities?

PHILLIP: Yes, we ended the year with a concentrated study and it was exciting. I guess it really started when I read *The Amish* by Doris Faber. It was such a perfect book for what ensued because it discussed the history and way of life of the Amish people and how and why they established their own communities. The students decided to research the history and development of our community.

Together we learned how the community was founded, the growth pattern, and where it got its name. In pairs or small groups, they studied the history of the school, various public buildings, the subdivisions, and so forth. They were amazed that the end of the old trolley line was in front of our school and talked about how they wished the trolley still existed and wondered why it didn't. They learned that our school was first a high school and then a junior high before becoming an elementary school and tried to find clues of the former inhabitants. After pulling together as much history of the community as we could, the students decided we should build our own community, a perfect community for the future. This was their idea, and with my blessings and enthusiasm behind them, they organized the class and began. They decided to work in groups of four to plan the community. They developed guidelines for transportation, utilities, housing, and businesses; they drew a plan of the community and described it in narrative. They researched and designed waste disposal systems, monorails, and other forms of transportation and alternative kinds of housing.

I was really pleased with what happened in this TI, and it was great fun being a member of this learning community. I was especially pleased with their determined efforts to suggest various things that might be done to improve the quality of life for *all* members of a community. When the groups gave their final reports, other class members asked excellent questions, and it was evident that their comments were based on real understanding. It sounded like a roomful of engineers engaged in building model communities. Come to think of it, they may have been designing their future community.

Fourth Grade: Ginny Blackburn, Jody Brewer, Ann Dominick, and Sherry Parrish

We've known Ginny, Jody, Ann, and Sherry for years and we consider them great teachers. Many teachers get along well with one another and their cooperation enhances their learning environments. But these four teachers are exemplary models for that cooperative spirit. What a pleasure to step into their classes and feel their camaraderie. While all four teachers are outstanding, each brings different strengths to the classroom.

Alabama history is included in the required curriculum for one semester of fourth grade in all Alabama schools and is a subject that should be of interest to nine- and ten-year-olds. Ginny, Jody, Ann, and Sherry have taught the required half-year of Alabama history for years, but they were never satisfied with the children's response or with the textbook and other materials provided by the state. They decided to work together and try something different, but they weren't sure what. As they discussed the different possibilities, the Civil War kept coming up as the area students had the most questions about and seemed the most interested in. Since this war played such a major role in the history of the state, they decided a TI on the Civil War was the way to approach the required study. Short on materials but long on ideas and enthusiasm, they decided to do the TI at the same

Sherry Parrish, Ginny Blackburn, Ann Dominick, and Jody Brewer plan for their Civil War TI.

time so they could not only plan together but support each other as the TI developed.

Our first question is, when did you find time to work together?
ANN: We eat lunch together every day, which gives us a chance to share ideas, and we chat frequently before and after school and whenever we get a chance. We're friends so we talk a lot anyway.

Because you worked closely together, did the TIs in each room look the same?
ANN: We really enriched the TI when we put our heads, hearts, talents, children, and resources together. It's amazing, though, how different the same TI looked in our four classrooms. For example, one class went much further with Reconstruction than the others, and one class became much more involved with dramatization than other classes. My class was shocked by the large number of soldiers who died of disease and became interested in exploring the health conditions of the soldiers during the war. Jody's class, on the other hand, was intrigued by the number of teenagers who fought in the war.

How did you each start the TI?

GINNY: I began the same way I do with every TI. We brainstormed and kids reported everything they knew about the Civil War. They had false ideas about Abraham Lincoln. Some kids thought that the South had won the war and that the South loved Lincoln. Many were unsure about who won the war, but they all loved Lincoln.

JODY: I always have my students write down what they know about a topic. This lets them know how much they already know, and it provides me with information about their prior knowledge as well as their point of view and their opinions about a particular topic. I ask them later to refer back to what they wrote in the beginning so they can see how much they have learned and how their opinion about something or someone may have changed.

SHERRY: My students also brainstormed everything they knew about the Civil War. We listed everything that interested them. In small groups, they categorized the list into subheadings. They chose from the list the subtopic they wanted to study. At least two people, and no more than four, had to select the same topic. A couple of students came up with a topic that wasn't on the original list.

ANN: I almost always begin a TI by having the class list what they know about the topic and what they would like to know. They knew very little about the Civil War. They had some sketchy information and a lot of misconceptions. They mixed up the songs "Yankee Doodle" and "The Battle Hymn of the Republic," for example. They just didn't have the prior knowledge about this topic to ask their normally intelligent questions.

Since the children seemed to have less prior knowledge on this topic than on others, what did you do to build background?

GINNY: I think we all did some of the same things. Since the students needed information before they could go off on their own, we told stories, read historical fiction, and shared picture books about the war. The students, too, helped build background by sharing things they learned from their parents each evening.

I'm a storyteller so naturally I used my talent in this area to spark interest and build background, and I enjoy telling stories as much as the kids enjoy listening to them. I'm also a trivia buff on the Civil War so I used trivia facts to spark interest and stimulate reading.

Great! Tell us what happened when the students began their research.

SHERRY: My students were in six research groups: battles, ammunition, important people, Ku Klux Klan, Underground Railroad, and the

Ginny Blackburn gives information on Civil War heroes.

army. There were four students in each group, and everyone was in what I call a core group that represented one member from each group. The core group met every few days to share what their own groups had learned and then reported other groups' learning to their group. I didn't have a lot of reporting by students in front of the class, so having the core groups meet was a way of keeping everyone informed about what the research groups were learning.

JODY: We waited several days before they picked the topics they wanted to research. They then selected their own groups, which were Underground Railroad, famous people, weapons, battles, civilians during the war, and Reconstruction. I met with each group to support their research and to suggest important points they might want to learn more about. After I knew each group was going in the right direction, I left them alone and made myself available for individual or group consultation.

ANN: My students listed questions that focused on issues and organized the questions under topics to form their committees. The committees we ended up with were issues that caused the war, people who fought battles, the home front, and furniture. I added architecture to the list because I'm especially interested in antebellum homes.

Jody Brewer reads aloud to her students, which builds students' knowledge and interest.

GINNY: I generally have committees that work on topics, but this time they all wanted to research their own topics. They read and shared trade books. They found wonderful historical fiction but complained that they couldn't find enough books with pictures of the Civil War. They really learned a lot and just never seemed to finish sharing.

We know that you devoted much of the day to this TI. Would anyone care to tell us how you spent the day?

ANN: Except for the time on my math program and science, the whole day was spent on the Civil War. With some TIs that have more science connections, I incorporate science into the TI. I always have math, although I integrate as much math in the TI as is natural. There was some math in this TI, such as figuring the costs of feeding and clothing the army and the costs of ammunition.

JODY: We started our day with the TI to make sure it wouldn't get pushed aside. I began the day by reading aloud from a biography or a historical fiction book related to the Civil War. The groups always met in the morning and usually again in the afternoon to continue their research. There was at least one research time during the day when everyone dug for information, which was followed by a discussion of what they had learned. Like Ann, I had a separate math and science class. (Ginny and Sherry nodded that they had also had separate math and science classes.)

How did you ensure that all of your students were doing reading and writing?

JODY: I required them to read trade books about the Civil War, but they could choose from lots of different ones. After they finished a book, there were book talks about how their feelings or opinions changed as they read and listened to others tell about their books. For their research, they had to read from several sources. My students wrote a lot on their research project, but I also asked them to write diary entries. I wanted them to be either someone who was left at home, a soldier, or a famous person. They had choices and their diary entries showed that they were thinking about the war and its effects.

ANN: My kids read historical fiction and biographies of Civil War figures. I try to have them write in the same genre most appropriate for the TIs, and for the Civil War historical fiction and biography were perfect. Reading and writing about people and their lives brought history alive, and the students were more emotionally involved with this TI than my classes in the past.

You have all mentioned literature and seem excited that historical fiction played such a major role in this particular TI. Were there any special books that helped bring this period alive and evoked exciting discussions?

GINNY: *Jump Ship to Freedom* by James and Christopher Collier. I almost tried to discourage a child from reading this book, but decided not to and was I glad I didn't. It's so difficult to find literature that reflects attitudes of other times and is still appropriate for today's society. This book is, of course, controversial primarily because of the authors' choice to use the word "nigger," which I find extremely offensive. This book, however, led to a very thoughtful discussion about why the Colliers chose to use the word, the word itself, racial bias, stereotyping, and the origin of offensive words for other ethnic groups.

SHERRY: Our absolute favorite was Ann Petry's book, *Harriet Tubman, Conductor on the Underground Railroad*. This book, which I read aloud, created so much excitement in our room. Some had heard the term "underground railroad" and thought it was an underground train. They had no idea of the human element, the reason for the "railroad," or who was involved. They had so many questions that I couldn't answer. They wanted to know more about the author, to know more books on the Underground Railroad and Harriet Tubman. Our whole TI could have been built around this one book.

Sherry Parrish conducts a conference on a trade book this student has just read.

JODY: Slavery was a big issue in my room, too. My students were simply appalled as they read *The Slave Dancer* by Paula Fox. They couldn't believe that some people, even preachers, felt that God thought whites were superior to blacks. This book is also controversial, and I tried, through class discussion, to bring out how the book might have been different if told from the point of view of one or more of the slaves.

ANN: Since Ginny, Sherry, and Jody have mentioned books about slavery, I'll recommend one, too. My students loved hearing the slaves' first person narratives from Julius Lester's book, *To Be a Slave*. Another book I must mention, though, is Irene Hunt's *Across Five Aprils*. This one really hit home as the children started thinking about their own families and the consequences if one member had fought for the Confederates and another for the Union Army.

You said that you shared resource people. Would you tell us about that?

GINNY: There were so many, but one that especially touched my students was an older African American man from the community who knew Martin Luther King, Jr. He talked about how slavery had ended many years ago but how there are still injustices. He

Janie Holmes, a resource teacher, speaks to students about the civil rights struggle.

discussed being in the civil rights march in Selma. He also recalled times before the civil rights movement when African Americans were in real danger in certain areas if their car broke down or if they needed to buy gas. He discussed segregated restaurants and the first sit-ins in downtown Birmingham.

SHERRY: My students and I especially enjoyed a talk by one of the teachers in our building, Mrs. Janie Holmes, who teaches Chapter I. She had grown up during the civil rights era and had marched with Dr. Martin Luther King, Jr. She described what it was like growing up in the South. Because the students respect her so much as a teacher and a person, they felt free to ask her questions. In an open discussion, she told them that many people's attitudes hadn't changed much and made connections between the Rodney King incident in Los Angeles and the civil rights movement.

We got another resource person in my room just by accident. One day the physical education teacher came into the room to see me about changing the PE schedule and overheard the weapons committee as they discussed guns and ammunition. Before long, he was diagramming things about guns on the board and became a resource person in all the classes.

ANN: We found a woman in the community who had a collection of clothes, bullets, canteens, and buttons from the time of the Civil War. She brought replicas of some of the clothes and the kids got to examine them. They were fascinated that there were no zippers. The kids also enjoyed handling the guns, sabers, and swords. I was nervous about it, but I'm glad they had the experience.

We haven't asked yet what nonprint media were helpful.

GINNY: We showed the movie *Iron Clad Ship*, and there was a filmstrip on Harriet Tubman that the students seemed to enjoy. Oh, yes, they liked the Civil War songs that a local musical group, Three on a String, had recorded.

What were some expressive forms used by the students to show they had a good understanding of the topic?

SHERRY: In this TI, it was probably the reports that the students gave on the books they had read. You wouldn't believe how much they identified with the characters in the books. My kids made some great posters and performed super skits, but it was their book projects that impressed me.

JODY: My groups all decided how they would share their knowledge, and I felt that all of them reflected good understanding. Their expressions took a lot of different forms, including reenactments of battle scenes, skits with costumed characters like Robert E. Lee, models of battlefields, and a Jeopardy-style game about the Civil War.

ANN: The students enjoyed debating between classes. It was unbelievable how heated these debates were. They had to decide, if you were living at that time, what side you'd be on. After a debate, the kids could change to the other side. I was surprised that they could argue so well for both sides.

Jody, earlier you mentioned how you view your role as a TI teacher. Is there more that you would care to say?

JODY: I'm not sure how others see themselves, but I see my role as that of a facilitator. I want kids to construct their own beliefs through discussion and reading good literature. I let their beliefs emerge, but I give direction when needed. Some groups need guidance while others need little. I try to be a skillful questioner so I can encourage the generation of ideas.

You said that you each brought different strengths to the TI that made it richer. Would you talk about that?

SHERRY: I'd like to answer that one. Ann is a folksinger and she brought her guitar and taught many of the Civil War songs to all the classes.

Ann Dominick sings Civil War songs with the students.

Ginny weaves magic as a storyteller and shared so many stories with our classes that helped build prior knowledge and brought the study to life. Jody has an incredible knowledge of historical fiction and biography, and she helped us all learn about new books. I guess my strength would have to be in sharing the files of stuff on the Civil War that I've collected.

All of you used TIs this past year. What are some of the differences between using TIs and textbooks?

SHERRY: It takes time to do a TI and it's a lot easier to just go by the book. TIs force me to tune in to the topic, focus on the children, and be a real learner. I like the feeling of being another learner in the classroom and not just a giver of information.

ANN: When I followed a textbook, it was difficult for me to spark interest. In a TI, the interest is there from the very beginning and intensifies throughout the study.

JODY: I've never used a textbook much. The thing I don't like about textbooks is that students don't seem to get a sense of what history is really about, and especially the role people play.

My African American parents were especially pleased that I didn't use a regular textbook to teach the Civil War. They complimented me on how I handled the topic; they realize that historical fiction truly gets at how horrible slavery was and that most textbooks skim over the conditions. Oops! I've got to mention another book. We read *Which Way Freedom* by Joyce Hansen, which is the story of a young runaway slave who joined the Union Army.

Are there any differences in what your students learn and the insights they have when you use a TI rather than a textbook approach?

GINNY: When you use a TI, your students develop their own point of view. In the process, they argue and change sides and sometimes even straddle the fence.

SHERRY: With a TI, the responses students give reflect a much deeper commitment to an issue. For the first time, the kids looked beyond surface issues like who fought where and when in the battles. They got at the heart of the matter, that is, social issues and causes. They delved into slavery and they understood the idea of states' rights and how that played a part in the Civil War. With TIs, content takes on a personal meaning for them. One of the best things we did was to incorporate all the historical fiction based on the issues of the Civil War into the TI. My students felt on a personal level with the children and the families who went through the war. When you teach by TIs, both you and the children have a much deeper and richer experience.

Fifth Grade: Naomi Goss

Naomi follows a traditional curriculum in terms of required subjects, but that's where tradition stops. She's a true lover of children's literature, a continuous learner, and a risk taker. Each of these attributes is evident as she guides her students toward becoming independent researchers and socially conscious human beings. Anyone who thinks that students today are only interested in designer tennis shoes should visit Naomi's class. They would find a very deep level of social consciousness among these fifth graders, who research topics that interest them.

You do lots of TIs in your class. How are the topics selected and how do you proceed?

NAOMI: For students who to want to engage in research, I know I must follow their interests. We talk about "hot topics" in different

Naomi Goss guides a discussion with her students.

curriculum areas, things they're interested in, and we go from there. During the first two weeks of school, we spend a lot of time at the nearby public library studying and learning how to use the *Readers' Guide to Periodical Literature*. I initially establish certain guidelines for their research. For example, they must ask three questions they want to answer about a topic, they must use a magazine article and a reference book other than an encyclopedia, and they must conduct an interview to gather information for their reports. I constantly refer to the book *The I-Search Paper* by Ken Macrorie (1988) as I help guide their writing.

What were some of the "hot topics" this year?
NAOMI: One of the hot topics in health was AIDS. The kids were really curious and popping with questions. I told them I had been learning about the legal issues related to AIDS and education. While they explored answers to their questions, I continued to study the legal issues. They asked questions and I asked questions. We had some really thoughtful class discussions.

Another topic I hadn't planned and in which we learned a lot about government, legal issues, and caring about each other was abuse. I was reading aloud *Cracker Jackson* by Betsy Byers, and the class discussion started going all over the place about abuse and what constitutes abuse and what can be done about it. I knew one of my students was a victim of abuse, but he had never talked about it and I certainly hadn't expected him to. When I finished the book, though, he actually told the whole class his story. Those fifth graders handled this issue in such a caring way and their research papers showed a sensitivity not usually openly exhibited by children this age.

Another TI in which I learned a lot about the thinking of these fifth graders was one that followed the reading of *Tuck Everlasting* by Natalie Babbitt. Their questions revolved around issues that I thought only adults, or certainly much older students, thought about. Their I-Search papers were about their philosophy of life, life and death, and the consequences of living forever. They wrote essays on springs, on land and ownership, and what might happen in their lifetimes if they lived to be over one hundred.

On one of our visits to your room, you were reading Mildred Taylor's Roll of Thunder, Hear My Cry *and, at one point in the story, the children all clapped and cheered because "justice had been done." Were you reading that book as part of a TI?*

NAOMI: Actually I was reading it for several reasons. I often read books in advance of a required topic; historical fiction is a must for social studies topics. I love Mildred Taylor's work, and her books not only provide background knowledge, they get the kids emotionally involved before we begin our required study of civil rights. I say "required study" and it is, but it was the longest and most active of our TIs this year. I didn't follow the curriculum guide and didn't go back as far in time as we're supposed to in fifth grade, but my conscience is clear because so many good things happened in our study and, as a result, lots of people in Alabama know this class. They became real civil rights advocates.

Tell us some highlights of that TI.

NAOMI: Since you mentioned *Roll of Thunder, Hear My Cry*, I'll start with that. I also think that book inspired students' concern about civil rights and everyone being treated equally in society. They compared and contrasted—one of the skills on our continuum [she smiles]—the school for black children and the school for white children as described in the book. They then talked about how our school is different and how some things are still the same. There had been a lot in the newspaper about changing tax laws in Alabama so more

Naomi Goss's students listen to each other, share information, and make suggestions to one another.

money would be available in poor counties. They wrote letters to the legislators about inequalities and told them that no child should have to use discarded textbooks or attend school in August in non-air-conditioned buildings. They talked about the importance of class size and the need for money for supplies and books for the library. I personally delivered the letters when I joined a parent march on the capitol asking for more money for education.

Your student teacher, Suzanne Binderman, told us that your students even did some writing about the Ku Klux Klan.

NAOMI: Yes, Suzanne was really surprised when a group she was working with wanted to interview Klan members but decided against it because they were afraid, and asked her if she knew anyone or could help them find somebody who knew a Klan member. Suzanne said she wished the KKK did not exist in Alabama, but thought they could find someone who had been a member. Well, they did. They found older relatives and some community members who knew people who had belonged to the Klan. The surprising thing to Suzanne, though, was that they didn't come back talking about the activities of the Klan but about their families, and their writing was about how family members are not responsible for other members of their family and how it isn't fair to blame a whole family for one member's racial prejudice. I must say that much of the credit was due to Suzanne's skillful questioning and guidance.

Birmingham was such an important city during the civil rights movement in the sixties. Did you do much with that during the TI?

NAOMI: Birmingham became the center of attention when we were reading a biography of Martin Luther King, Jr., and there were a lot of references to Birmingham. Their questions started coming and they wanted to know more and more. Through a friend, I located two ministers and a public official who had been involved in civil rights during the sixties and were recently involved in helping establish our wonderful new Civil Rights Institute in Birmingham. They agreed to talk to the class, and my students and I were spellbound as our guests talked about organizing marches, and how Martin Luther King, Jr., had told them to put their weapons in their hats and how he preached nonviolence as a way of obtaining civil rights. They told of sit-ins at lunch counters and how difficult it was to remain calm when fire hoses and dogs were directed at the marchers. Through the powerful words of the guests, these students will long remember the civil rights events of the sixties and will take a deeper interest and appreciation with them as they visit Birmingham's newest museum and know their city played an important role in the struggle for civil rights.

We know that all of your TIs aren't about such sensitive issues as you've described and that these issues aren't a normal part of most fifth-grade curricula. Are there some uncertainties on your part?

NAOMI: Certainly, but I don't let that stop me from doing what I think is best for my students. I sometimes feel pulled between the TI topics and the demands of the curriculum and then I remind myself that I *am* addressing the curriculum, but I'm doing so in a way that makes sense for me and the children. There are some topics that I don't have a great deal of information or knowledge about beforehand, but I admit it and tell the students that I'll learn right along with them. And then, of course, within many TIs there are controversial issues, and I have to be sensitive to the feelings and attitudes of the students, their parents, and my colleagues. In the end, though, I have to say that it's all worth it. I enjoy my teaching and take a great deal of satisfaction as I see my students developing responsibility for their own learning and growing in their understanding of the world.

Amanda Kutz's student places flags in a military cemetery.

Sixth Grade: Amanda Kutz

Amanda Kutz, a former student of ours, teaches sixth grade at Laurel Bay School in Beaufort, South Carolina. All the students in the school are Navy or Marine dependents and represent many cultures and ethnic groups. Because of their parents' different post assignments, a lot of the students know a great deal about different parts of the world. We

Amanda Kutz's students visiting one of many historic sites.

were fascinated by the local history TI we observed when we visited Amanda's class.

Amanda, tell us what you know about how this local history study began.
AMANDA: The person who came up with the idea was the media specialist, Cecile Dorr. She is a former social studies teacher and wants all students to be as excited about history as she is. Mr. Davis, the principal, also supported us in many ways. He developed a brochure listing all the historical sites in the area.

Who all was involved with the project?
AMANDA: A lot of people. Everyone who had anything to do with sixth grade: the sixth-grade teachers, the art teacher, the computer specialist, and the music teacher, and, of course, Mrs Dorr, the media specialist. The project was even supported by the Commandant of the Marines, who stresses the strengthening of family. This TI enhanced family togetherness as members read during a family reading time, traveled to historical sites as a family, and collaborated on the various projects associated with the TI.

What went on in your classroom during the local history TI?

AMANDA: Since I'm the language arts teacher, students did a lot of reading and writing in my class. During this TI, I focused on literature from the Beaufort area. I read aloud local ghost stories, and there are some terrific ones, like "Land's End Light," "Frogmore Manor," "Baynard Hall," and "Lady in Blue." The kids loved them and wrote their own ghost stories.

We saw illustrations of Gullah tales on the walls as we came into your room. Tell us about them.

AMANDA: I believe that the best way to know a time or place is through literature. As you may know, Gullah stories are part of the African American culture of Beaufort. We read Gullah tales and the students illustrated some of the stories. They also wrote plays based on Gullah stories and performed them for other classes. In music, the students studied how George Gershwin copied Gullah music and watched a video of his great musical, *Porgy and Bess.*

You said the art teacher was involved. In addition to the illustrations we saw in your room, were there other art activities?

AMANDA: Absolutely. The students, for example, made beautiful stained glass windows out of paper with designs similar to designs in the old churches and houses in Beaufort.

Just how did the computer specialist help with the TI?

AMANDA: Mr. Davis is not just an ordinary computer specialist. He taught them to do desktop publishing. He helped with a newsletter on local history and helped students design the letterhead stationery we used for writing letters. I can't praise him enough for the help he gave two of my students as they analyzed some local plantation records that were kept over a century ago. With his guidance, they did spreadsheets from the records and displayed graphs that showed the amount of crops produced and sold.

We haven't mentioned math yet.

AMANDA: Math wasn't as integrated with the TI as the other subjects, but there was some involvement. For example, they figured the mileage to different historical sites.

We met Jim Smith, the social studies teacher, when we went with you on the walking tour of historical Beaufort. How does he relate social studies to the TI?

AMANDA: In Jim's class, each student selected a historical site to research. Parents got really involved and took their kids to the sites and worked with them on the study. Not surprisingly, a lot of the boys loved to study the forts and anything related to the military.

We've discussed most of the curriculum areas except for science. We heard part of the presentation by the guest from the State Fish and Wild Life Department as he spoke on the different water habitats in the area.

AMANDA: We brought lots of outside speakers in during the local history TI. That speech, especially, generated a lot of interest The kids really got into reptiles and insects after he spoke, and began to make connections between local history and science.

What did your parents have to say about the study?

AMANDA: They were pleased that their kids were so excited about it, and they seemed to enjoy learning right along with them. As you know, Beaufort is steeped in history, so it made for a rich study for parents as well as for their children.

How long did the TI last?

AMANDA: In the beginning, we said that it would last for eight weeks, but it lasted three weeks longer. There were several neat activities that kept interest in the topic. For example, one mother came in and made Frogmore stew. Simply delicious. Had it been left up to the kids, the TI would have gone on longer, but we hope their interest in local history will continue.

What did you especially like about teaching local history?

AMANDA: Without question, it was the excitement of the students. I didn't see a bored kid for weeks. That's unusual for sixth grade

Special Education: Debra Rust

Debra Rust is a special education resource teacher who serves children in grades one through four. She has a passion for saving the earth and tries to instill that in all her students. Debra is an active member of the Sierra Club, serves on the board of Ruffner Nature Center, works with the Alabama Conservancy, and belongs to a number of national environmental organizations. She has visited many places of natural beauty, her favorites so far being Africa and the Amazon rain forest. With her interest in nature, it's no wonder that she has a Saving the Earth TI every year. It was during this TI several years ago that The B.A.T. Club was formed. In this interview we focused on the B.A.T. Club rather than on the Saving the Earth TI from which the club emerged.

Debra, we want to know about the B.A.T. Club and the bat study part of your Saving the Earth TI.

DEBRA: First, let me tell you where I got my interest in preserving bats, because I remember exactly. It was at the annual meeting of the Alabama State Conservancy in 1987 when I heard Dr. Merlin Tuttle, head of the Bat Conservation International with headquarters in

Debra Rust shows the records for the B.A.T. Club, which are kept in this suitcase.

Austin, Texas. Dr. Tuttle told how fruit-eating bats in the tropics are essential seed-dispersing animals and are necessary for the pollination of tropical trees. He went on to tell us that the rain forests would be seriously threatened without them. Dr. Tuttle and his pet bat, Yuri, got me interested in bat preservation, and this interest has increased and intensified over the years.

I left the Alabama Conservancy meeting all fired up and could hardly wait to tell my students what I had learned. It didn't take much to ignite their interests. They had become strong environmental activists, and this fit right into our TI on saving the earth. We began our study of bats and Richard Mills, our local chiropotologist, or bat expert, became our mentor. He suggested books and other resources and we devoured them. We became bat experts. We took a field trip to the Birmingham zoo where Mr. Mills presented a bat program for us. Mr. Mills was amazed by the children's knowledge about bats and their high interest level.

After weeks of immersing ourselves in a study of bats, the students wanted to join the Bat Conservation International. You can imagine the excitement of the youngsters when we received

FIGURE 8-1: B.A.T. *Club membership card*

our membership card and started getting the monthly publications that gave us updated information.

Tell us how the B.A.T. *Club began.*

DEBRA: Soon after we joined the Bat Conservation International Janie, a third grader, suggested that we form a bat club so we could start saving bats in Alabama. The other students jumped with excitement and started to brainstorm a name for our club. After lively discussion, they agreed upon B.A.T. Club (Bats Aren't Terrible; Bats Are Terrific).

Janie was elected president and guidelines for the group were developed. Within a few days, the students had established two major objectives for the club: (1) to educate ourselves and others about bats, and (2) to promote the conservation of bats among members of our school and the general public.

It wasn't long until someone suggested that we could make money by selling memberships to our club; we settled on fifty cents for each membership. As the discussion rolled along, another child pointed out that we needed membership cards if we were going to sell memberships. What would go on the card? During our week-long discussion about the card, I called a friend of mine in Maine, Peter Parnall, who is a well-known children's author and illustrator with a strong interest in environmental issues. I explained our latest episode about the bats and the need for a membership card, and he said, "Let me design the bat for their membership card." Within a few days, several sketches of bats arrived and the children selected the one they liked best (see Figure 8-1).

The cards are given to people when they buy a membership. We now have over a thousand members, including Peter Parnall and the NBC "Today" show's Willard Scott. The membership fees give us money for our bat conservation work. In addition to earning money from the membership sales, we sell bumper stickers the

Midfield Bat Club

FIGURE 8-2: B.A.T. *Club bumper sticker*

students designed and one of our parents helped to get printed (see Figure 8-2).

It sounds as if your students are really excited about the club and preserving bats. What are some of the club's activities?

DEBRA: The students work hard to spread the word about bats. In the beginning, we only provided programs on bats for other classes in our school. Now, however, in addition to doing presentations at our school, we travel to other schools and groups as far away as fifty miles. The students were especially thrilled when they were asked to do one at the local Sierra Club and the Audubon Society. They just recently spoke to a large group comprised of the Midfield Board of Education and community members, who were astonished by the children's fervor and knowledge. The students told them the world could be overrun with insects if bats aren't saved and that our oxygen supply will be depleted if there aren't bats to pollinate the trees. They backed up their statements with statistics and additional information.

We know that you want your students to get involved in the political process.

DEBRA: Yes, I do, and my students have become very politically involved in issues involving bats. For example, when the students learned that there were plans to develop land near Lake Purdy, a lake near Birmingham, they became concerned. They knew that the numerous caves near the lake were nursery caves for the gray bat and that construction would negatively affect the bats. My students and a large number of other club members wrote letters to the mayor and the city council of Birmingham asking them to reconsider their plans for development.

The B.A.T. Club didn't stop the development, but the political activists in our club were instrumental in getting the authorities to change the plans so that there was no construction near the caves. As a part of the compromise, special fences were put up around the caves so that people couldn't go in and disturb the bats.

Tyler Alexander hangs a bat house as club members watch.

We're really impressed with the political activism of your students. Is there anything else you'd care to tell us about the club's activities?

DEBRA: You recall that I said we earn money through memberships and the sale of bumper stickers. We use most of the money to buy bat houses, which we place around the community. So far, we have bat houses at our local nature center, and at the zoo, and we recently placed one at Camp Sequoyah, a Boy Scout camp near Birmingham. We buy the bat houses from the Bat Conservation International and follow their instructions for locating them.

We know that many in our area have become aware of the B.A.T. Club and their activities.

DEBRA: It's been gratifying that my students have received recognition for their conservation efforts. A couple of years ago we thought that President Bush was going to visit our club. When we learned that the President was scheduled to visit Birmingham, one of my students, Jonathan Nabors, wrote him a letter (Figure 8-3).

We received word that the President would visit us. As you can imagine, the children were absolutely thrilled. We learned later, however, that plans had changed and he would not be able to visit our club while in Birmingham. The change in plans did create quite

> Dear Mr. President:
>
> Mrs. Rust's class at Midfield Elementary School welcomes you to Birmingham, Alabama. We are inviting you to be an honorary member of the Midfield Bat Club. We hope you are concerned about bats because bats are an important part of our environment.
>
> Bats are interesting creatures and sometimes have funny facial expressions. Bats have the same number of bones in their wing that we have in our hand.
>
> We invite you to come and see us. If you are able to come, we could show you our bat slides and the bat houses we donate to different organizations. Would you like a bat house for the White House? Maybe we could donate a bat house for you to take home. We hope to see you soon.
>
> Sincerely,
> Jon Nabors

FIGURE 8-3: *Letter to President Bush*

a stir locally. *The Birmingham News*, for example, printed an editorial saying that President Bush should have visited us and that he owed us an apology.

The children were disappointed, of course, that the President didn't visit, but this didn't put a damper on their enthusiasm for bat conservancy. The club and its members have since received many honors and awards. Tyson Alexander, for example, was nominated by his first-grade teacher to receive the *Weekly Reader* Jefferson Award for outstanding community service. Tyson had presented more bat programs to classrooms, churches, and other groups than any other member of the club and had sold the most memberships. We were all delighted when he won the national contest. He received a trip to Washington, D.C., and met Mrs. Bush and Millie.

FIGURE 8-4: *Article in "Weekly Reader" about B.A.T. Club*

When he was in Washington, the editors of Weekly Reader interviewed him and were impressed with Tyson and the story he told. They later sent a reporter to Birmingham to interview him about the B.A.T. Club and an article about Tyson and the club appeared in the Weekly Reader (see Figure 8-4).

As a result of the Weekly Reader article, the Silver-Burdett Publishing Company sent a film crew to make a video of the B.A.T. Club entitled We Kids Can, which is being seen by kids across the country.

Where are you now as far as the club is concerned?

DEBRA: Where are we now? The club meets twice a month and members still show a strong interest in bat conservation. I emphasize bats for two weeks during each school year, at which time old and new members concentrate on bat study. Guess what? I learn something, too, each time. Let me end my interview about the B.A.T. Club by sharing a rap my kids just finished:

Rust's Class Rap

We are Ms. Rust's class,
The best in the nation.
We fight for conservation.

We started the bat club
To help our friends the bats.
Anyone who harms a bat
Is nothing but a rat.

We fight against billboards.
They are all around town.
If we had a hatchet
We'd love to chop them down.

Sure we're only kids
But we're trying to save our land,
So why don't you chip in
And lend a hand?

Dreaming: Portrait of a Theme Immersion

9

In the first eight chapters, we've relied primarily on the written word to describe theme immersions and to convey their benefits, and to demonstrate how this process might be applied in your classroom. In this concluding chapter, we supplement the narrative of the first eight chapters with a photographic essay to help you focus on and summarize in your own mind the essence of what we've said.

As we were compiling this chapter, we learned anew the wisdom of the old saying, "a picture is worth a thousand words." At their best, pictures bring ideas to life, focus attention, sharpen perceptions, enhance understanding, arouse emotions, and encourage sensitivity. We hope these pictures of Sonia Carrington and her fifth-grade students as they immerse themselves in dreams and dreaming accomplish some of the same things for you. We hope the pictures stimulate an emotional, intellectual, and professional commitment to a process we're convinced can give new meaning and relevance to the lives of teachers and young people—theme immersion.

The children's interest in dreaming began when Brad read aloud the book he wrote about dreams.

Students find that dreams are everywhere. Who wouldn't be fascinated with dreaming and the imagination?

What's the topic for our next theme immersion? Suggestions range from Mardi Gras to hunger in Africa, but dreams continue to dominate the discussion.

The webbing of ideas about dreams is spontaneous. Sonia contributes information about the Aborigines' religion and Dreamtime that she learned from her Australian brother-in-law.

The students list everything they know about dreams and brainstorm questions they have about the topic.

Sonia helps students narrow down the subtopics to be given to the committees. Many subtopics relate to dreams, but four dominate.

Who serves on which committee? To make sure there is no favoritism in the selection process, students draw names.

Students sign their name beside their committee choice.

Each committee begins to work on the chosen subtopic.

Where do young researchers find the information they need? They use many sources.

Move over, Barbara Walters! Sonia demonstrates how she interviews people to collect information.

Brad conducts a telephone interview with Sonia's brother-in-law from Australia, who is knowledgeable about Aborigines and Dreamtime.

Sonia also helps students who are tracking down information on the Aborigine dream picture.

High tech can go a long way toward putting research on the fast track. Here, a student uses a CD-ROM to find information.

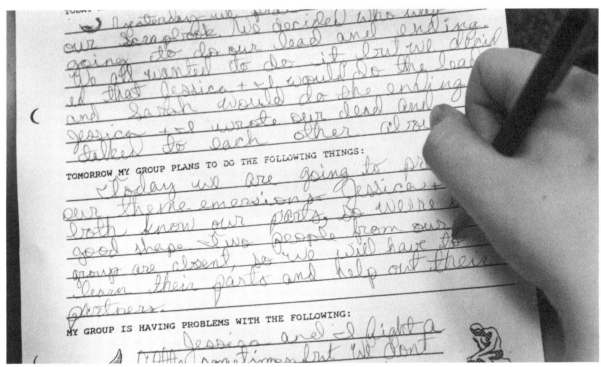

At least twice a week, students prepare a group progress report.

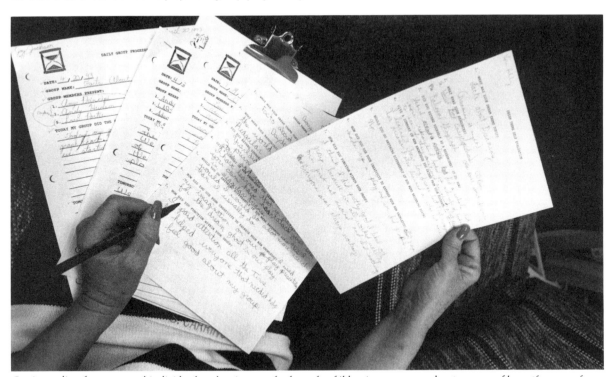

Sonia studies the group and individual evaluations to check on the children's progress and note any problems they may have.

Students continue to search for information on their subtopics.

"Auntie Litter," whose dream is to stamp out littering, talks to the class.

Why do we dream? The children hear what a psychologist has to say during a classroom visit.

Group reporting time. The "Ways Imagination Is Used" committee discusses the dreams of famous people.

The "Aborigine" committee reports on what they've learned.

The "Facts About Dreaming" committee shares interesting findings.

The "Famous Dreamers" committee tells how the world can be a better place.

Group evaluation is an important part of the overall evaluation process.

Each student completes a self-evaluation form. It's a great way for students to get a better understanding of how they learn.

A student selects items for his portfolio.

Did it all go according to plan? What Sonia learns in this evaluation conference will help her prepare for the next time the class tackles a theme.

Sonia reflects on the dream TI. She believes her students learned to respect the ideas and opinions of others as they collaborated on a topic that really mattered to them. They refined their ability to do research and learned a great deal about dreams and the power of imagination and hope.

References

Professional Books

ANTHONY, ROBERT J., TERRY D. JOHNSON, NORMA I. MICKELSON, and ALISON PREECE. 1991. *Evaluating Literacy: A Perspective for Change.* Portsmouth, NH: Heinemann.

CAMBOURNE, BRIAN. 1988. *The Whole Story: Natural Learning and Acquisition of Literacy in the Classroom.* New York: Ashton Scholastic.

DEWEY, JOHN. 1910. *My Pedagogic Creed.* Chicago: A. Flanagan Company.

DEWEY, JOHN. 1915. *Democracy and Education.* New York: Macmillan.

DEWEY, John. 1938. *Experience and Education.* New York: Macmillan.

Getting Started in Science: A Blueprint for Elementary School Science Education. 1989. Washington, DC: National Center for Improving Science Education.

GOODMAN, DEBRA. 1992. "My Gradebook." In *The Whole Language Catalog: Supplement on Authentic Assessment*, ed. Kenneth Goodman, Lois Bridges Bird, and Yetta Goodman. Santa Rosa, CA: American School Publishers, 114–115.

GOODMAN, KENNETH. 1970. "Behind the Eye: What Happens in Reading." In *Reading: Process and Program*, ed. Kenneth Goodman and Olive S. Niles. Urbana, IL: National Council of Teachers of English, 3–38.

GOODMAN, KENNETH. 1986. *What's Whole in Whole Language.* Portsmouth, NH: Heinemann.

GOODMAN, KENNETH. 1992. "The Case of the Vanishing Checklists." *The Whole Language Catalog: Supplement on Authentic Assessment*, ed. Kenneth Goodman, Lois Bridges Bird, and Yetta Goodman. Santa Rosa, CA: American School Publishers, 110.

GOODMAN, KENNETH, E. BROOKS SMITH, ROBERT MEREDITH, and YETTA GOODMAN. 1987. *Language and Thinking in School: A Whole Language Curriculum.* Katonah, NY: Richard C. Owen.

GOODMAN, YETTA. 1978. "Kid Watching: An Alternative to Testing." *National Elementary School Principal* 57: 41–45.

GOODMAN, YETTA, DOROTHY WATSON, and CAROLYN BURKE. 1987. *Reading Miscue Inventory*. Katonah, NY: Richard C. Owen.

GRAVES, DONALD. 1983. *Writing: Teachers and Children at Work*. Portsmouth, NH: Heinemann.

GRAVES, DONALD. 1992. "Portfolios: Keep a Good Idea Growing." In *Portfolio Portraits*, ed. Donald Graves and Bonnie Sunstein. Portsmouth, NH: Heinemann, 1–12.

GRAVES, DONALD, and BONNIE SUNSTEIN, eds. 1992. *Portfolio Portraits*. Portsmouth, NH: Heinemann.

IRWIN, JOHN. 1982. *Baskets and Basket Makers in Southern Appalachia*. Exton, PA: Schiffer.

JAROLIMEK, JOHN. 1967. *Social Studies in Elementary Education*. New York: Macmillan.

MACRORIE, KEN. 1988. *The I-Search Paper*. Portsmouth, NH: Boynton/Cook.

MANNING, MARYANN, and GARY MANNING. 1991. "The Case for Theme Immersion." *Teaching K–8* 22: 55–57.

PIAGET, JEAN. 1963. *The Psychology of Intelligence*. Paterson, NJ: Littlefield, Adams, and Company.

PIAGET, JEAN. 1964. *Judgment and Reasoning in the Child*. Paterson, NJ: Littlefield, Adams, and Company.

ROUTMAN, REGIE. 1991. *Invitations*. Portsmouth, NH: Heinemann.

SMITH, FRANK. 1971. *Understanding Reading*. New York: Holt, Rinehart, and Winston.

SMITH, KAREN. 1992, August. *Inquiry Based Teaching: Making Meaning, Creating Worlds*. Paper presented at the meeting of the Whole Language Umbrella Association, Niagara Falls, New York.

VYGOTSKY, L. S. 1978. *Mind in Society: The Development of Higher Order Psychological Processes*, ed. Michael Cole, Vera John-Steiner, Sylvia Scribner, and Ellen Souberman. Cambridge: Harvard University Press.

VYGOTSKY, L. S. 1987. *The Collected Works of L. S. Vygotsky*, ed. Robert W. Rieber and Aaron S. Carton. New York: Plenum.

WATSON, DOROTHY, ed. 1987. *Ideas and Insights: Language Arts in the Elementary School*. Urbana, IL: National Council of Teachers of English.

WELLS, GORDON. 1986. *The Meaning Makers: Children Learning Language and Using Language to Learn*. Portsmouth, NH: Heinemann.

Children's Books

BABBITT, NATALIE. 1975. *Tuck Everlasting*. New York: Farrar, Straus & Giroux.

BAYLOR, BYRD. 1975. *The Desert Is Theirs*. New York: Scribner.

BAYLOR, BYRD. 1986. *I'm in Charge of Celebrations*. New York: Scribner.

BUNTING, EVE. 1991. *Fly Away Home*. New York: Clarion.

BYERS, BETSY. 1985. *Cracker Jackson*. New York: Viking.

COHLENE, TERRI. 1990. *The Dancing Drum*. Vero Beach, FL: Rourke.

COLLIER, JAMES, and CHRISTOPHER COLLIER. 1981. *Jump Ship to Freedom*. New York: Delacorte.

FABER, DORIS. 1991. *The Amish*. New York: Doubleday.

FOX, PAULA. 1973. *The Slave Dancer*. Scarsdale, NY: Bradbury.

GEORGE, JEAN CRAIGHEAD. 1972. *Julie of the Wolves*. New York: Harper and Row.

GIBBONS, GAIL. 1986. *Up Goes the Skyscraper*. New York: Winds Press.

GIBBONS, GAIL. 1990. *How a House Is Built*. New York: Holiday House.

HANSEN, JOYCE. 1986. *Which Way Freedom*. New York: Walker

HUNT, IRENE. 1986. *Across Five Aprils*. New York: Pacer Books for Young Adults.

JEFFERS, SUSAN. 1991. *Brother Eagle, Sister Sky*. New York: Dial.

LESTER, JULIUS. 1968. *To Be a Slave*. New York: Dial.

PETRY, ANN L. 1955. *Harriet Tubman: Conductor on the Underground Railroad*. New York: Crowell.

TAYLOR, MILDRED. 1976. *Roll of Thunder, Hear My Cry*. New York: Dial.

WILDER, LAURA INGALLS. 1953. *Little House in the Big Woods*. New York: Harper and Row.

Resource Section
Annotated Bibliography

Professional Books

ATWELL, NANCIE, ed. 1989. *Coming To Know: Writing to Learn in the Intermediate Grades.* Portsmouth, NH: Heinemann.

The book is an excellent resource for teachers who want to emphasize writing across the curriculum. Chapters written by teachers of grades 3 through 6 explain how students write in various content areas. In addition to providing ideas on using writing to learn in the content areas, Atwell gives suggestions for using children's literature in content areas.

BARCHERS, SUZANNE, and PATRICIA MARDEN. 1991. *Cooking Up U.S. History.* Englewood, CO: Teachers Ideas Press.

Cooking is a valid classroom activity and often results from research about a particular region or cultural group. This book contains recipes reflecting the practices of several periods of American history. The Library Link questions that follow many of the recipes may interest students in further research.

CALKINS, LUCY. 1994. *The Art of Teaching Writing,* New Edition. Portsmouth, NH: Heinemann.

Calkins provides insights about the teaching of writing and about teaching in general. This deeply personal book shows how writing can be used to help children make the world more understandable.

CORDEIRO, PAT. 1992. *Whole Learning: Whole Language and Content in the Upper Elementary Grades.* Katonah, NY: Richard C. Owen.

The whole language philosophy underlies every aspect of this book. Cordeiro explains how whole learning integrates various areas of the curriculum and shows how subjects can revolve around the same theme or concept in grade 3 to 6 classrooms.

CRAFTON, LINDA. 1991. *Whole Language: Getting Started . . . Moving Forward*. Katonah, NY: Richard C. Owen.

Crafton provides a theoretical basis for whole language teaching and offers numerous strategies for introducing getting started and extending whole language. She details basic practices for implementing whole language and provides resources for text sets, author sets, genre sets, and theme sets. The theme set section lists books under topics such as death, feelings, female protagonist, and peace.

EDELSKY, CAROLE, BESS ALTWERGER, and BARBARA FLORES. 1991. *Whole Language: What's the Difference?* Portsmouth, NH: Heinemann.

The authors give a clear explanation of whole language, address theoretical constructs, and compare whole language with other progressive movements. This book demonstrates that whole language is much more than a label; it is a perspective, a philosophy. There is a brief but excellent discussion of differences between thematic units and thematic topics (pp. 64–68).

FORESTER, ANNE, and MARGARET REINHARD. 1991. *On the Move*. Winnipeg: Peguis.

The authors provide an in-depth explanation of how to implement reading and writing workshops. In addition, they show how to meet curriculum requirements in social studies, the sciences, and the arts. They give several specific examples of integration, such as an all-school unit on astronomy.

FURNISS, ELAINE, and PAMELA GREEN, eds. 1991. *The Literacy Connection: Language and Learning Across the Curriculum*. Armadale, Australia: Eleanor Curtain.

Fourteen teachers and teacher educators share their ideas about language across the curriculum. Topics explored include science, math, drama, computers, and literature. The authors show how teachers support students as they use literacy to learn in various subject areas.

GAMBERG, RUTH, WINNIEFRED KWAK, MEREDITH HUTCHINGS, and JUDY ALTHEIM, with GAIL EDWARDS. 1988. *Learning and Loving It: Theme Studies in the Classroom*. Portsmouth, NH: Heinemann.

The authors provide a definition of theme study and give basic guidelines, such as selecting a theme and identifying resources. The book is filled with practical suggestions for theme study and shows through case studies how it works.

GOODMAN, KENNETH, LOIS BRIDGES BIRD, and YETTA GOODMAN, eds. 1991. *The Whole Language Catalog*. Santa Rosa, CA: American School Publishers.

A comprehensive book on whole language with more than 500 contributors from around the world. Several of the articles in this volume deal with themes. One article, for example, recommends several books on thematic teaching on the topics of architecture, dragons, and peace.

GRAVES, DONALD. 1989. *Investigate Nonfiction*. Portsmouth, NH: Heinemann.

Graves provides an abundance of ideas on nonfiction writing, including making the transition from oral forms to reading and writing. Graves offers practical suggestions or "actions" for teachers to use with their students: interviewing, recording data, making reports, reading information sources, and examining the world around them.

HARWAYNE, SHELLEY. 1992. *Lasting Impressions: Weaving Literature into the Writing Workshop*. Portsmouth, NH: Heinemann.

Harwayne's passion for using good literature with children permeates the entire book. When literature is the core for the writing workshop and the entire curriculum, it can make lasting impressions on students' lives and on their writing.

HAYDEN, CARLA D., ed. 1992. *Venture into Cultures: A Resource Book of Multicultural Materials and Programs*. Chicago: American Library Association.

As the title indicates, this is a resource book about various cultures and includes annotated bibliographies of children's books and other materials for learning about ethnic groups found in significant numbers in the United States. The groups are African American, Arabic, Asian, Hispanic, Jewish, Native American, and Persian. The activities and programming ideas are helpful in generating ways of expressing knowledge during a theme immersion.

The Horn Book Guide. Boston: The Horn Book, Inc.

Published twice a year by *The Horn Book, The Horn Book Guide* includes short, critical annotations of all hardcover children's books published in the United States within a six-month period. Books are rated from outstanding to unacceptable. Especially useful to TI teachers are the Subject Index and the Series Index. The guide is $50.00 per year and may be ordered from: The Horn Book, Inc., 14 Beacon Street, Boston, MA 02108.

KATZ, LILLIAN G., and SYLVIA C. CHARD. 1989. *Engaging Children's Minds: The Project Approach*. Norwood, NJ: Ablex.

This book for early childhood teachers gives the theoretical principles of the project (topic or theme) approach and suggests ways of implementing it. Katz and Chard suggest several topics, such as the local community and local events and current affairs. In a project approach, teachers identify key events, such as field trips, guest speakers, and learning activities for individual children or groups.

KOBRIN, BEVERLY. 1988. *Eyeopeners*. New York: Penguin.

Over 500 nonfiction books are reviewed, underscoring the idea that nonfiction books are essential in children's education. The first few chapters are filled with suggestions for teachers, parents, and librarians. In the rest of the book, Kobrin annotates nonfiction books under topics such as buildings, children on their own, and divorce.

LIDDELOW, LORELEI. 1990. *Cook with Me*. Winnipeg: Peguis.

The author gives simple cooking activities along with related plays, games, stories, and poems that can enhance language development. In food moods, for example, one of the nine themes, Liddelow gives a recipe for animal cookies accompanied by a play depicting animal friendship.

MACRORIE, KEN. 1988. *The I-Search Paper*. Portsmouth, NH: Boynton/Cook.

Although the book was written for college students, many middle grade teachers find it useful in guiding their students as they explore questions and develop written reports. Students who develop an I-Search paper use their curiosity and their resources to validate their search, and write about their findings in a way that's interesting for them and for their readers.

MOSS, JOY F. 1990. *Focus on Literature*: A *Context for Literacy Learning*. Katonah, NY: Richard C. Owen.

This book for elementary and middle school teachers provides units for studying literature in the classroom. The units include extensive bibliographies of high quality literature and offer structure and strategies for building a literature-rich curriculum.

PAPPAS, CHRISTINE C., BARBARA Z. KIEFER, and LINDA S. LEVSTIK. 1990. *An Integrated Language Perspective in the Elementary School*. White Plains, NY: Longman.

The authors explain integrated language theory and give many examples to show how the theory is translated into classroom practice. The text includes six fully explained thematic units at different elementary grade levels, each with a web that shows various aspects of the unit. A detailed schedule shows an hour by hour and day by day time frame and lists teacher and student activities. Each unit concludes with a suggested bibliography of children's literature.

RIEF, LINDA. 1992. *Seeking Diversity*: *Language Arts with Adolescents*. Portsmouth, NH: Heinemann.

Rief, a middle school language arts teacher, shares her teaching and organizational techniques. The book is filled with practical ideas for implementing reading and writing workshops in a traditional junior high school setting. In one chapter, Rief describes a unit on the elderly and shows how she and the students read literature and make connections in their own writing.

ROUTMAN, REGIE. 1991 *Invitations: Changing as Teachers and Learners* K–12. Portsmouth, NH: Heinemann.

The book truly *invites* readers to reflect on their teaching and provides a great many specific suggestions for improving teaching and learning. Chapter 12, Integration, is particularly pertinent for teachers interested in thematic units.

SAUL, WENDY, and SYBILLE A. JAGUSCH, eds. 1991. *Vital Connections: Children, Science, and Books.* Portsmouth, NH: Heinemann.

The book includes articles by educators, editors, literature and science specialists, and children's authors such as Jean Craighead George. It shows how children can connect with science through trade books in ways that are difficult with a basal science text. It emphasizes the importance of science literature for children.

SLAPIN, BEVERLY, and DORIS SEALE, eds. 1992. *Through Indian Eyes the Native American Experience in Books for Children.* Philadelphia, PA: New Society Publishers.

In the preface, the editors note that they may have 'spoiled some people's favorite books" by pointing out racism and bias in books with Native American characters. This is true, but they certainly give back an excellent resource. TI teachers will find the articles and book reviews thought-provoking and insightful. The book also includes a checklist for evaluating children's books about Native Americans, addresses for obtaining curriculum materials prepared for Native American educators, a selected bibliography of books by and about Native Americans, and an annotated bibliography of Native American authors for young readers.

THOMPSON, GARE. 1991. *Teaching Through Themes.* New York: Scholastic Professional Books.

The first part of the book gives several general suggestions on theme teaching, including when to theme teach and where to find themes. The rest of the book offers specific guides for teaching six themes—people, friendship, habitats, courage, mystery, and survival—and suggests several books with accompanying activities for each theme.

TUNNELL, MICHAEL O., and RICHARD AMMON, eds. 1993. *The Story of Ourselves: Teaching History Through Children's Literature.* Portsmouth, NH: Heinemann.

The chapters are written by educators and trade book authors such as Pam Conrad. The book offers guidance and suggestions for teachers who want to use children's literature in their social studies program. In addition to the practical suggestions for bringing history alive with children's books, there is a comprehensive bibliography of trade books about North American history.

WELLS, GORDON, and GEN LING CHANG-WELLS. 1992. *Constructing Knowledge Together*. Portsmouth, NH: Heinemann.

In a three-year study of teachers in four schools in inner-city multilingual communities, the authors investigated how teachers can ensure that all children achieve the goals of literacy. Through the collaborative project, teachers created classrooms in which children used literacy to learn about topics that interested them and to share their information with others.

Professional Journals/Magazines

BASKWILL, JANE. 1988."Themestorming." *Teaching K–8*, 19: 80–82.

Baskwill, a Canadian primary-grade teacher, says that a good theme must be rich in literature (both fiction and nonfiction) and have natural links to several areas of the curriculum. If a theme is to develop, the teacher must make certain that children have enough time to become immersed in it. Themestorming (brainstorming and webbing the different aspects for the theme study) lets teacher and students see the relationships between parts of the theme study.

COWENS, JOHN. 1992. "Spider Sniffing." *Teaching K–8*, 22: 42–45.

Cowens, a fourth-grade teacher in Oregon, explains a unit in his classroom that integrates natural science, physical science, and language arts. In their study, the children read fiction and nonfiction books about spiders, observe spiders and spider webs, and conduct experiments on these amazing creatures. The author-teacher describes several fascinating activities during the unit.

FREEMAN, VALDORAY Y. 1987. "Do-It-Yourself History." *Teaching K–8*, 18: 61–62.

Freeman shares her excitement about a local history project she has implemented in her school for several years. She describes a field trip to the local historical museum and how a display theme inspired the children to create a miniature display of their own depicting the life of the Siwanoys, the city's earliest settlers. Other activities include studying pictures of the community's early years and hearing guest speakers, such as a former governor, who visited the class and talked about early state government.

GALDA, LEE, and JANET COTTER. 1992. "Children's Books: Exploring Cultural Diversity." *The Reading Teacher*, 45: 452–460.

The authors group the books for this article under the theme of cultural diversity. As they point out, however, many of them could be incorporated within studies of history or geography or grouped within thematic units on topics such as sibling rivalry or growing up. In the introduction to their review of the books, they emphasize the importance of including books about a variety of cultures, so that cultural variety becomes a basic part of the entire curriculum rather than a unit topic alone.

GENSER, LILLIAN. 1985. "Children's Rights and Responsibilities: A Teaching Unit for the Elementary Grades." *Social Education*, 49: 500–503.

The activities in this unit are assigned and directed by the teacher, rather than student-directed and student-selected, as in a TI. But the article contains many ideas a TI teacher could use. For example, "Have students tell the stories of books they have recently read. Ask about the characters' rights and responsibilities." Genser gives an address for getting materials on human rights: Center for Peace and Conflict Studies, Wayne State University, Detroit, MI 48202. As a part of the unit of study, each child receives a copy of "The Declaration of the Rights of the Child," written by a committee of the United Nations in 1959. The Declaration is reprinted in the article.

GREENE, LYNDA. 1991. "Science-Centered Curriculum in Elementary School." *Educational Leadership*, 49: 42–46.

A report on a project in schools in California that attempted to connect science in engaging ways with other subjects. Teachers use science as the conceptual focus for instruction in reading, social studies, arithmetic, and so on.

JIBILIAN, JARY. 1987. "Good Morning Moscow." *Teaching K–8*, 17: 46–51.

Jibilian shares her ideas about one of the teaching units she uses with her seventh graders, a study of the former Soviet Union. She discusses how she, as a language arts teacher, collaborated with the social studies teacher on the unit. A final activity was to make a television production of students' findings modeled on the format of "Good Morning America."

JIBILIAN, JARY, and JEANNE MARTEL. 1987. "Writing for Tomorrow." *Teaching K–8*, 17: 47–49.

The authors, a language arts teacher and a reading teacher, explain how they worked together to implement a unit on women's rights, censorship, and sex stereotyping in their eighth-grade classes. They describe some of the unit activities and include a list of the books they read and discussed, such as *Dick and Jane As Victims: Sex Stereotyping in Children's Readers*, *Inherit theWind*, and *The Day They Came to Arrest the Book*.

KEREKES, JOANNE. 1987. "The Interdisciplinary Unit . . . It's Here to Stay." *Middle School Journal*, 18: 12–14.

Kerekes, a unit leader at her middle school, shares the story of interdisciplinary units, which began several years ago at her school. She suggests that teachers should educate parents and students about units, select topics that are interesting for both students and teachers, keep costs to a minimum, and make sure there are grade-level teams, a common planning time, and block scheduling. Some of the units she mentions are law and order, propaganda, the changing family, and heroes.

MANNING, MARYANN, and GARY MANNING. 1991. "The Case for Theme Immersion." *Teaching K–8*, 21: 55–58.

The article forms the basis for this book, *Theme Immersion*. The authors differentiate between theme units and theme immersion. Students and teacher investigate a topic or theme that leads them into many other disciplines. Skills develop as students explore a particular theme. Included in the article are ideas for themes, identifying topics, brainstorming, constructing a web, gathering information, and expressing ideas.

STRUBBE, MARY A. 1990. "Are Interdisciplinary Units Worthwhile? Ask Students!" *Middle School Journal*, 21: 36–38.

Student evaluations of interdisciplinary units indicate that they enjoyed them and liked working closely with each other on interesting and challenging topics. By analyzing students' responses and their own observations, the author concludes that successful interdisciplinary units should include relevant topics; clear goals and objectives; variety in topics, structures, activities, and groupings; choice in topics, projects, and groupings; adequate time; processes and/or products; field trips; group cooperation; sharing; and community involvement.

Resource Section
Literature for Selected Theme Immersions

The books in this bibliography have been recommended by theme immersion teachers or have received acclaim in critical reviews. The books, for the most part, have been published since 1989. We've included several topics found in school textbooks and courses of study in addition to those we think would make interesting TIs. Grade level designations are given in brackets at the end of the entry: P = Primary; I = Intermediate; MS = Middle School.

ANIMAL ABUSE

Popcorn Park Zoo: A House with a Heart by Wendy Pfeffer. New York: Messner, 1992. [I]

Shiloh by Phyllis Reynolds Naylor. New York: Atheneum, 1991. [I]

Stuffer by Peter Parnall. New York: Macmillan, 1992. [P]

APARTHEID

At the Crossroads by Rachel Isadora. New York: Greenwillow, 1991. [MS]

Chain of Fire by Beverly Naidoo. New York: Lippincott, 1990. [MS]

The Land and People of South Africa by Jonathan Paton. New York: Lippincott, 1991. [MS]

Nelson Mandela: The Fight Against Apartheid by Steven Otfinoski. Highland Park, NJ: Mill Brook Pr., 1992. [MS]

Nelson Mandela: Voice of Freedom by Libby Hughes. Minneapolis: Dillon, 1992. [I]

THEMBA by Margaret Sacks. New York: Lodestar, 1992. [I]

ARCHITECTURE

Frank Lloyd Wright by Yona Zeldis McDonough. New York: Chelsea, 1991. [MS]

Houses and Homes by Ann Morris. New York: Lothrop, 1992. [MS]

Julia Morgan by Cary James. New York: Chelsea, 1990. [MS]

Lebek: A City of Northern Europe Through the Ages by Xavier Hernandez and Jordi Ballonga. Boston: Houghton Mifflin, 1991. [I]

A Memorial for Mr. Lincoln by Brent Ashabranner. New York: Putnam, 1992. [MS]

The Random House Book of How Things Were Built by David J. Brown. New York: Random House, 1992. [I]

ASTRONOMY

The Big Dipper by Franklin M. Branley. New York: HarperCollins, 1991. [P]

The Constellations: How They Came To Be by Ray A. Gallant. New York: Four Winds, 1991. [MS]

The Earth and Sky by Gallinard Jeunesse and Jean-Pierre Verdet. New York: Scholastic, 1992. [P]

If You Lived on Mars by Melvin Berger. New York: Lodestar, 1989. [I]

My Place in Space by Robin Hirst and Sally Hirst. New York: Orchard, 1992. [I]

Neptune by Seymour Simon. New York: Morrow, 1991. [I]

Our Solar System by Seymour Simon. New York: Morrow, 1992. [I]

Planetary Exploration Series by Don Davis et al. New York: Facts on File Publisher, 1990. [MS]

Space Words: A Dictionary by Seymour Simon. New York: HarperCollins, 1991. [I]

CIVIL RIGHTS

Coretta Scott King: Keeper of Dreams by Sandra Henry and Emily Taitz. Hillside, NJ: Enslow, 1992. [MS]

Freedom of the Press by J. Edward Evans. Minneapolis, MN: Lerner, 1990. [I]

Freedom Songs by Yvette Moore. New York: Orchard, 1991. [MS]

Great African American Series by Patricia McKissack and Fredrick McKissack. Hillside, NJ: Enslow, 1991. [P]

Just Like Martin by Ossie Davis. New York: Delacorte, 1992. [I]

Let Freedom Ring: A Ballad of Martin Luther King, Jr. by Kathy Kristensen Lambert. New York: Chelsea, 1992. [I]

Marion Wright Edelman: Defender of Children's Rights by Steve Otfinoski. Woodbridge, CT: Blackbirch, 1992. [I]

Mississippi Challenge by Mildred Pitts Walter. New York: Bradbury, 1992. [MS]

Rosa Parks: My Story by Rosa Parks with Jim Haskins. New York: Dial, 1992. [MS]

Who's to Know? Information, the Media, and Public Awareness by Ann E. Weis. Boston: Houghton Mifflin, 1990. [MS]

COUNTRIES OF AFRICA

Afro-Bets First Book about Africa by Veronica F. Ellis. Orange, NJ: Just Us Books, 1990 [P/I]

Ajeemah and His Son by James Berry. New York: HarperCollins, 1992. [I]

Botswana in Pictures edited by Thomas O'Toole. Minneapolis: Lerner, 1990. [MS]

The Day of Ahmed's Secret by Florence P. Heide and Judith H. Gilliland. New York: Lothrop, 1990. [P/I]

Desert December by Dorian Haarkoff. New York: Clarion, 1992. [P]

Egypt: Gift of the Nile by Arthur Diamond. Minneapolis, MN: Dillon, 1992. [I]

Elephants Calling by Katherine Payne. New York: Crown, 1992. [I]

The Fortune Tellers by Lloyd Alexander. New York: Dutton, 1992. [I]

Kenya: Africa's Tamed Wilderness by Joann J. Burch. Minneapolis: Dillon, 1992. [I]

Mali in Pictures edited by Thomas O'Toole. Minneapolis, MN: Lerner, 1990. [MS]

Masai and I by Virginia Kroll. New York: Four Winds, 1992. [P]

The Middle of Somewhere: A Story of South Africa by Sheila Gordon. New York: Orchard/Jackson, 1990. [I/MS]

Rehema's Journey: A Visit to Tanzania by Barbara A. Margolies. New York: Scholastic, 1990. [P/I]

Sundiata: Lion King of Mali by David Wisniewski. New York: Clarion, 1992. [P]

Somewhere in Africa by Ingrid and Niki Daly. New York: Dutton, 1992. [P]

When Africa Was Home by Isabel Wilner. New York: Dutton, 1991. [P]

The Year of the Leopard Song by Eric Campbell. San Diego: Harcourt Brace Jovanovich, 1992. [MS]

COUNTRIES OF ASIA

An Asian Tragedy: America and Vietnam by David Detzer. Brookfield, CT: Millbrook, 1992. [MS]

Children of China by Rajo. Minneapolis: Carolrhoda, 1990. [I]

The Chinese by Pamela Odijk. Morristown, NJ: Burdett, 1991. [I]

Indonesia: A Nation of Islands by Judy Jacobs. Minneapolis: Dillon, 1990. [I]

Indonesia in Pictures by Geography Department Editors. Minneapolis: Lerner, 1990. [MS]

The Journey of Meng by Doreen Rappaport. New York: Dial, 1991. [P]

Kanu of Kathmandu: A Journey in Nepal by Barbara A. Margolies. New York: Four Winds, 1992. [P]

The Land and People of Korea by S. E. Solberg. New York: HarperCollins, 1990. [MS]

The Land and People of Pakistan by Mark Weston. New York: HarperCollins, 1992. [MS]

Land of Yesterday, Land of Tomorrow: Discovering Chinese Central Asia by Brent Ashabranner. New York: Cobblehill, 1992. [MS]

Lion Dancer: Ernie Wasn't Chinese by Kate Waters and Madaline Slovenz-Low. New York: Scholastic, 1990. [P]

Vietnam: Rebuilding a Nation by Sherry Garland. Minneapolis: Dillon, 1990. [I]

COUNTRIES OF AUSTRALIA, NEW ZEALAND, AND THE SOUTH PACIFIC

Australia by Laura Dolce. New York: Chelsea, 1990. [MS]

Australia: A Lucky Land by Al Stark. New York: Dillon, 1992. [I]

Australia: On the Other Side of the World by Penny Stanley-Baker. Ossining, NY: Young Discovery Library, 1992. [I]

Dinosaurs Down Under: And Other Fossils from Australia. New York: Clarion, 1990. [MS]

My Place by Nadia Wheatley. Sydney: Kane/Miller, 1992. [I]

New Zealand in Pictures by Geography Department Editors. Minneapolis: Lerner, 1990. [MS]

Tasmania by Joyce Powzyk. New York: Morrow, 1987. [I]

This Place is Lonely by Vicki Cobb. New York: Walker, 1991. [P]

Wallaby Creek by Joyce Powzyk. New York: Morrow, 1985. [I]

Windows by Jeanie Baker. New York: Greenwillow, 1991. [P]

COUNTRIES OF CENTRAL AND SOUTH AMERICA

An Adventure in the Amazon by The Cousteau Society. New York: Simon, 1992. [I]

Argentina by Lol Liebowitz. New York: Chelsea, 1990. [MS]

Argentina: A Wild West History by Marge Peterson and Rob Peterson. Minneapolis: Dillon, 1990. [I]

Brazil by Evelyn Bender. New York: Chelsea, 1990. [MS]

Land and People of Bolivia by David Nelson Blair. New York: Lippincott, 1990. [MS]

Land and People of Venezuela by Geoffrey Fox. New York: HarperCollins, 1991. [MS]

Panama and the United States: Their Canal, Their Storm Years by Edward F. Dolan. New York: Watts, 1990. [MS]

A Picture Book of Simon Bolivar by David A. Adler. New York: Holiday, 1992. [P]

COUNTRIES OF THE MIDDLE EAST

Against the Storm (Turkey) by Gaye Hicyilmaz. Boston: Joy Street, 1992. [MS]

Iraq in Pictures by Geography Department Editors. Minneapolis: Lerner, 1990. [MS]

Iran by Sander Renfield. New York: Chelsea, 1990. [MS]

The Land and People of Turkey by William Spencer. New York: Lippincott, 1990. [MS]

When Will the Fighting Stop? A Child's View of Jerusalem by Ann Morris. New York: Atheneum, 1990. [I]

CRIME

Bob War and Poke by Harvey Watson. Boston: Houghton Mifflin, 1991. [I]

Checking on the Moon by Jenny Davis. New York: Orchard, 1991. [MS]

Violence on American Streets by Gene Brown. Brookfield, CT: Millbrook, 1992. [I]

Wild Iris Bloom by Mavis Jukes. New York: Knopf, 1992. [I]

CULTURES: AFRICAN AMERICAN

Arthur Ashe by Ted Weissberg. New York: Chelsea, 1991. [MS]

Billy the Great by Rosa Guy. New York: Delacorte, 1992. [P]

Black Dance in America: A History Through Its People by James Hoskins. New York: Crowell, 1990. [MS]

Charlie Parker Played Be Bop by Chris Raschka. New York: Orchard/Jackson, 1992. [P]

Cousins by Virginia Hamilton. New York: Philomel, 1990. [I]

Drylongso by Virginia Hamilton. San Diego: Harcourt Brace Jovanovich, 1992. [P]

Duke Ellington by Gene Brown. New York: Burdett, 1991. [MS]

Flying Free: America's First Black Aviators by Philip S. Hart. Minneapolis: Lerner, 1992. [I]

Jump at de Sun: The Story of Zora Neale Hurston by A. P. Porter. Minneapolis: Carolrhoda, 1992. [I]

Li'l Sis and Uncle Willie: A Story Based on the Life and Paintings of William H. Johnson by Gwen Everett. New York: Rizzoli, 1992. [P]

Martin Luther King, Jr. by Dianne Patrick. New York: Watts, 1990. [MS]

Now Is Your Time: The African American Struggle for Freedom by Walter Dean Myers. New York: HarperCollins, 1991. [MS]

Orin Bell by Barbara Hood Burgess. New York: Delacorte, 1991. [I]

Outward Dreams! Black Inventors and Their Inventions by Jim Haskins. New York: Walker, 1991. [MS]

The Road to Memphis by Mildred Taylor. New York: Dial, 1990. [MS]

Sojourner Truth: Ain't I a Woman? by Patricia and Fredrick McKissach. Hillsdale, NJ: Enslow. [I]

Tar Beach by Faith Ringgold. New York: Crown, 1991. [P]

Two Tickets to Freedom: The True Story of Ellen and William Craft, Fugitive Slaves by Florence B. Freedman. New York: Bedrick, 1989. [I]

CULTURES: ASIAN AMERICAN

El Chino by Allen Say. Boston: Houghton, 1990. [I]

Famous Asian Americans by Janet Nomur and Wendy Dunn. New York: Cobblehill, 1992. [I]

Finding My Voice by Marie G. Lee. Boston: Houghton Mifflin, 1992. [MS]

Hoang Anh: A Vietnamese-American Boy by Diane Hoyt-Goldsmith. New York: Holiday, 1992. [P]

The Journey: Japanese Americans, Racism, and Renewal by Sheila Hamanak. New York: Orchard/Jackson, 1990. [I]

The Moon Bridge by Marcia Savin. New York: Scholastic, 1992. [I]

My Name is San Ho by Jayne Pettit. New York: Scholastic, 1992. [I]

Roses Sing on New Snow: A Delicious Tale by Paul Yee. New York: Macmillan, 1992. [P]

Tales from Gold Mountain by Paul Yee. New York: Macmillan, 1990. [I/MS]

Tall Boy's Journey by Joanna Halpert Kraus. Minneapolis: Carolrhoda, 1992. [P]

CULTURES: HISPANIC AMERICANS

Abuela by Arthur Dorras. New York: Dutton, 1991. [P]

Baseball in April, and Other Stories by Gary Soto. San Diego: Harcourt Brace Jovanovich, 1990. [I/MS]

A Birthday Basket for Tia by Pat Mara. New York: Macmillan, 1992. [P]

Cesar Chavez by Bruce W. Conrad. New York: Chelsea, 1992. [I]

Family Pictures by Cuadros de Familia. Chicago: Children's Book Press, 1990. [P/I]

A Fire in My Hands: A Book of Poems by Gary Soto. New York: Scholastic, 1991. [I]

Maria: A Christmas Story by Theodore Taylor. San Diego: Harcourt, 1992. [I]

A Migrant Family by Larry Dane Brinner. Minneapolis: Lerner, 1992. [I]

Neighborhood Odes by Gary Soto. San Diego: Harcourt, 1991. [I]

Pacific Crossing by Gary Soto. San Diego: Harcourt, 1992. [I]

Roberto Clemente by Peter C. Bjarkman. New York: Chelsea, 1991. [I]

CULTURES: JEWISH

All the Lights in the Night by Arthur A. Levine. New York: Tambourine, 1991. [P]

Appleblossom by Shulamith Levey Oppenheim. San Diego: Harcourt Brace Jovanovich, 1991. [P]

Boys Here—Girls There by Riki Levinson. New York: Lodestar, 1992. [P]

Daddy's Chair by Sandy Lanton. Rockville, MD: Kar-Ben, 1991. [P]

Fancy Aunt Jess by Amy Hest. New York: Morrow, 1990. [P]

Goldie's Purim by Jane Breskin Zallben. New York: Holt, 1991. [P]

Grandma's Latkes by Malka Drucker. San Diego: Harcourt Brace Jovanovich, 1992. [P]

Hide and Seek by Ida Vos. Boston: Houghton Mifflin, 1991. [I]

The House on Walenska Street by Charlotte Herman. New York: Dutton, 1990. [I]

Leaving for America by Roslyn Bresnick-Perry. Chicago: Children's Book Press, 1992. [P]

Letters from Rifka by Karen Hesse. New York: Holt, 1992. [I]

Mrs. Katz and Tush by Patricia Palacco. New York: Bantam, 1991. [P]

The Lily Cupboard by Shulamith Levey Oppenheim. New York: HarperCollins, 1991. [P]

The Man from the Other Side by Uri Orlev. Boston: Houghton Mifflin, 1991. [MS]

One Little Goat—Had Gadya by Betsy Platkin Feutsch. Northvale, NJ: Aronson, 1990. [P]

CULTURES: NATIVE AMERICAN

The Ancient Cliff Dwellers of Mesa Verde by Caroline Arnold. New York: Clarion, 1992. [I]

An Indian Winter by Russell Freedman. New York: Holiday House, 1992. [I]

Black Star, Bright Dawn by Scott O'Dell. Boston: Houghton Mifflin, 1988. [I/MS]

Buffalo Hunt by Russell Freedman. New York: Holiday House, 1988. [I/MS]

The Cherokee Indians by Nicole Claro. New York: Chelsea, 1991. [I/MS]

The Cheyenne Indians by Liz Sonneborn. New York: Chelsea, 1991. [I/MS]

Children of the Maya by Brent Askabranner. New York: Putnam, 1986. [I/MS]

The Choctaw by Emilie Lepthien. Chicago: Children's Press 1987. [I]

How the Bird Tree Got Its Stripes by Freda Ahenakew. Saskatoon, Saskatchewan: Fifth Hauser, 1988. [P]

How Raven Brought Light to the People by Ann Dixon. New York: Macmillan, 1992. [P/I]

The Indian Way: Learning to Communicate with Mother Earth by Gary McLain. Santa Fe, NM: John Muir Publications, 1990. [I/MS]

An Indian Winter by Russell Freedman. New York: Holiday, 1992. [MS]

My Heart Soars by Chief Dan George. Vancouver: Hancock House, 1989. [I/MS]

The Naked Bear: Folk Tales of the Iroquois by Dirk Zimmer. New York: Morrow 1987. [P/I]

The Navajo Indians by Leigh Hope Wood. New York: Chelsea, 1991. [I/MS]

The People Shall Continue by Ortiz Simon. Chicago: Children's Book Press, 1988. [P/I]

The Seminole by Emilie Lepthien. Chicago: Children's Press, 1985. [I]

Sky Dogs by Jane Yolan. San Diego: Harcourt Brace Jovanovich, 1990. [P]

Spirits, Heroes, and Hunters from North American Indian Mythology by Marion Wood. New York: Schocken, 1987. [I/MS]

They Dance in the Sky: Native American Star Myths by Jean Guard and Ray Williamson. Boston: Houghton Mifflin, 1987. [I/MS]

Thirteen Moons on Turtle's Back: A Native American Year of the Moons retold by Joseph Bruchac and Jonathan London. New York: Philomel, 1992. [P/I]

The Whistling Skeleton: American Indian Tales of the Supernatural by George Bird Grinnell. New York: Four Winds, 1992. [I/MS]

DEATH

Another Christmas by Susan L. Roth. New York: Morrow, 1992. [P]

Bringing the Farmhouse Home by Gloria Whelan. New York: Simon, 1992. [P]

Coast to Coast by Betsy Byars. New York: Delacorte, 1992. [I]

The Day Before Christmas by Eve Bunting. New York: Clarion, 1992. [P]

The Falcon's Wing by Dawna Lisa Buchanan. New York: Orchard/Jackson, 1992. [I]

The Fortune Teller in 5B by Jane Breskin Zalben. New York: Holt, 1992. [I]

Ghost Song by Susan Price. New York: Farrar, Straus & Giroux, 1992. [P]

Love You Soldier by Amy Hist. New York: Four Winds, 1991, [P/I]

Missing May by Cynthia Rylant. New York: Orchard/Jackson, 1992. [I]

Skipping School by Jessie Haas. New York: Greenwillow, 1992. [MS]

Some of the Pieces by Melissa Madeuski. Boston: Little, Brown, 1991. [P]

Words of Stone by Kevin Henks. New York: Greenwillow, 1992. [I]

FOSTER HOME CARE

As Far as Mill Springs by Patricia Pendergraft. New York: Philomel, 1991. [I]

A Forever Family by Roslyn Banish and Jennifer Jordon-Wong. New York: Harper, 1992. [I]

Kinder Transport by Olga Levy Drucker. New York: Holt, 1992. [MS]

HANDICAPPED

The Bus People by Rachel Anderson. New York: Holt, 1992. [MS]

Cakes and Miracles: A Purim Tale by Barbara Diamond Goldin. New York: Viking, 1990. [P]

Carver by Ruth Yaffe Radin. New York: Macmillan, 1990. [I]

Dear Mr. Bell . . . Your Friend, Helen Keller by Judith St. George. New York: Putnam, 1992. [MS]

Elfwyn's Saga by David Wisniewski. New York: Lothrop, 1990. [P]

Enemy by Connie Jordan Green. New York: Margaret K. McElderry Books, 1992. [I]

A Guide Dog Grows Up by Caroline Arnold. San Diego: Harcourt Brace Jovanovich, 1991. [I]

Hannah by Gloria Whelan. New York: Knopf, 1991. [I]

Into the Dark by Nicholas Wilde. New York: Scholastic, 1990. [I]

Listen for the Singing by Jean Little. New York: Harper Collins, 1991. [I]

Mom's Best Friend by Sally Hobart Alexander. New York: Macmillan, 1992. [P]

Mom Can't See Me by Sally Hobart Alexander. New York: Macmillan, 1990. [I]

A Picture Book of Helen Keller by David Adler. New York: Holiday, 1990. [P]

HEALTH: AIDS/HIV

AIDS: How It Works in the Body by Lorna Greenberg. New York: Watts, 1992. [I]

AIDS: What Does It Mean to You? by Margaret O. Hyde and Elizabeth H. Forsyth. New York: Walker, 1990. [MS]

Children and the AIDS Virus: A Book for Children, Parents, and Teachers by Rosmarie Hausherr. New York: Clarion, 1989. [P]

Come and Sit by Me by Margaret Merrifield. Toronto: Women's Press, 1990. [P]

Does AIDS Hurt? Educating Young Children About AIDS. Santa Cruz, CA: ETR Associates, 1992. [P]

Fighting Back: What Some People Are Doing About AIDS by Susan Kuklin. New York: Putnam, 1989. [MS]

For Our Children: A Book to Benefit the Pediatric AIDS Foundation. New York: Disney, 1991. [P]

Impacts of AIDS by Ewan Armstrong. New York: Watts, 1990. [MS]

Know About AIDS by Margaret O. Hyde and Elizabeth H. Forsyth. New York: Walker, 1990. [I/MS]

Losing Uncle Tim by MaryKate Jordan. New York: Albert Whitman, 1989. [P]

Magic Johnson: Champion with a Cause by Keith Elliot Greenburg. Minneapolis: Lerner, 1992. [I]

Ryan White: My Own Story by Ryan White and Ann Marie Cunningham. New York: Dial, 1991. [MS]

Teens with AIDS Speak Out by Mary Kittridge. New York: Messner, 1992. [I]

Two Weeks with the Queen by Morris Gleitzman. New York: Putnam, 1991. [I]

Z's Gift by Neal Starkman. Seattle: Comprehensive Health Education Foundation, 1988. [P/I]

HEALTH: ALLERGIES

Allergies: What They Are, What They Do by Judith S. Seixas. New York: Greenwillow, 1991. [I]

Lumps, Bumps, and Rashes by Alan E. Nourse. New York: Watts, 1990. [I]

HEALTH: ALZHEIMER'S DISEASE

A Beautiful Pearl by Nancy Whitelaw. Morton Grove, IL: Whitman, 1991. [P]

The Memory Box by Mary Bahr. Morton Grove, IL: Whitman, 1992. [P]

Sachiko Means Happiness by Kimiko Sakai. Chicago: Children's Press, 1990. [P]

HEALTH: ASTHMA

Asthma by Mona Kerby. New York: Watts, 1989. [MS]

Thin Air by David Getz. New York: Holt, 1990. [I]

HEALTH: SUBSTANCE ABUSE

Drug Abuse A–Z by Gilda Berger and Melvin Berger. Hillside, NJ: Enslow, 1990. [MS]

Drug Wars by Margaret O. Hyde. New York: Walker, 1990. [MS]

Know About Drugs by Margaret O. Hyde. New York: Walker, 1990. [MS]

Know About Smoking by Margaret O. Hyde. New York: Walker, 1990. [MS]

HISTORY: CIVIL WAR

Barbara Fritchie by John Greenleaf Whittier. New York: Greenwillow, 1992. [P]

The Battle of Gettysburg by Alden R. Carter. New York: Watts, 1990. [I]

Behind the Blue and Gray: The Soldier's Life in the Civil War by Delia Ray. New York: Lodestar, 1991. [MS]

Cadets at War: The True Story of Teenage Heroism at the Battle of New Market by Susan Provost Beller. Crozet, VA: Shoe Tree, 1991. [I]

Cecil's Story by George Ella Lyon. New York: Orchard, 1991. [P]

Civil War! America Becomes One Nation by James T. Robertson, Jr. New York: Knopf, 1992. [I]

Frank Thompson: Her Civil War Story by Bryna Stevens. New York: Macmillan, 1992. [I]

Gentle Annie: The True Story of a Civil War Nurse by Mary Francis Shura. New York: Scholastic, 1991. [I]

Jayhawker by Patricia Beatty. New York: Morrow, 1991. [I]

Jefferson Davis by Perry Scott King. New York: Chelsea, 1990. [MS]

The Long Road to Gettysburg by Jim Murphy. New York: Clarion, 1992. [I]

Marching Toward Freedom: Blacks in the Civil War. 1861–1865 by James McPherson. New York: Facts on File, 1991. [MS]

A Nation Torn: The Story of How the Civil War Began by Delia Ray. New York: Lodestar, 1990. [MS]

Red Cap by G. Clifton Wesler. New York: Lodestar, 1991. [MS]

A Separate Battle: Women and the Civil War by Ina Chang. New York: Lodestar, 1990. [MS]

Thunder at Gettysburg by Patricia Lee Gauch. New York: Putnam, 1990. [P]

Undying Glory by Clinton Cox. New York: Scholastic, 1991. [I]

HISTORY: COLONIAL AMERICA

Daily Life: A Sourcebook on Colonial America, edited by Carter Smith. Brookfield, CT: Millbrook, 1991. [MS]

The Explorers and Settlers: A Sourcebook on Colonial America, edited by Carter Smith. Brookfield, CT: Millbrook, 1991. [MS]

Governing and Teaching: A Sourcebook on Colonial America, edited by Carter Smith. Brookfield, CT: Millbrook, 1991. [MS]

Thomas Jefferson: The Revolutionary Aristocrat by Milton Meltzer. New York: Watts, 1992. [MS]

HISTORY: PIONEERS

Araminta's Paint Box by Karen Ackerman. New York: Atheneum, 1990. [P]

The Borning Room by Paul Fleischman. New York: HarperCollins, 1991. [MS]

Brother Moose by Betty Levin. New York: Greenwillow, 1990. [I]

Buffalo Soldiers by Robert H. Miller. New York: Burdett, 1991. [I]

Calamity Jane: Her Life and the Legend by Doris Faber. Boston: Houghton Mifflin, 1992. [I]

Going West by Jean Van Leeuwen. New York: Dial, 1992. [P]

Laura Ingalls Wilder: A Biography by William Anderson. New York: HarperCollins, 1992. [I]

Lawman of the Old West by James L. Collins. New York: Watts, 1990. [I]

Snowshoe Thompson by Nancy Smiler Levinson. New York: HarperCollins, 1992. [P]

Warm as Wool by Scott Russell Sanders. New York: Bradbury, 1992. [P]

HISTORY: REVOLUTIONARY WAR

The Battle of Lexington and Concord by Neil Johnson. New York: Four Winds, 1992. [I]

Katie's Trunk by Ann Turner. New York: Macmillan, 1992. [P]

This Time, Tempe Wick? by Patricia Lee Gauch. New York: Putnam, 1992. [I]

HISTORY: U.S. DEPRESSION

Boys Here—Girls There by Niki Levenson. New York: Lodestar, 1992. [P]

Grandpa's Mountain by Ruth Yaffe Radin. New York: Macmillan, 1992. [I]

Red-Dirt Jessie by Anna Myers. New York: Walker, 1992. [I]

HISTORY: VIETNAM WAR

America and Vietnam: The Elephant and the Tiger by Albert Marrin. New York: Viking, 1992. [MS]

America's Vietnam War: A Narrative History by Elizabeth Becker. New York: Clarion, 1992. [MS]

An Asian Tragedy: America and Vietnam by David Detzer. Brookfield, CT: Millbrook, 1992. [MS]

Portrait of a Tragedy: America and the Vietnam War by James A. Warren. New York: Lothrop, 1990. [MS]

The Purple Heart by Marc Talbert. New York: HarperCollins, 1992. [I]

The Wall by Eve Bunting. New York: Clarion, 1990. [P]

HISTORY: WORLD WAR I

Alex, Who Won the War by Chester Aaron. New York: Walker, 1991. [MS]

Along the Track by Tamar Bergman. Boston: Houghton Mifflin, 1991. [MS]

The Fire-Kaiser by Maurice Gee. Boston: Houghton Mifflin, 1992. [I]

Good-Bye, Billy Radish by Gloria Skurzynski. New York: Bradbury, 1992. [MS]

The Kingdom by the Sea by Robert Westall. New York: Farrar, Straus & Giroux, 1992. [I]

HISTORY: WORLD WAR II

All Those Secrets of the World by Jane Yolen. Boston: Little, Brown, 1991. [P]

But No Candy by Gloria Houston. New York: Philomel, 1992. [P]

The Christmas Box by JoAnne Stewart. New York: Knopf, 1992. [P]

Don't You Know There's a War On? by James Stevenson. New York: Greenwillow, 1992. [P]

In the Eye of War by Margaret Chang and Raymond Chang. New York: Margaret K. McElderry, 1990. [I]

The Lily Cupboard by Shulamith Levey Oppenheim. New York: HarperCollins, 1992. [P]

My Daddy Was a Soldier: A World War II Soldier by Deborah Kogan Ray. New York: Holiday House, 1990. [P]

Navajo Code Talkers by Nathan Aasing. New York: Walker, 1992. [I]

Pearl Harbor: America Enters the War by Terry Dunnahoo. New York: Watts, 1991. [MS]

The Promise by Robert Westall. New York: Scholastic, 1991. [MS]

Randolph's Dream by Judith Mellecker. New York: Knopf, 1991. [P]

Shadow of the Wall by Christa Laird. New York: Greenwillow, 1990. [MS]

The Sky Is Falling by Kit Pierson. New York: Viking, 1990. [I]

Stepping on the Cracks by Mary Downing Hahn. New York: Clarion, 1991. [I]

Strange but True Stories of World War II by George Sullivan Walker. New York: Walker, 1991. [I]

Waiting for Anya by Michael Morpurgo. New York: Viking, 1991. [I]

War Boy: A Country Childhood by Michael Foreman. New York: Arcade, 1990. [I]

When Mama Retires by Karen Ackerman. New York: Knopf, 1992. [P]

World War II Fiftieth Anniversary Series by Wallace B. Black and Jean F. Blashfield. New York: Crestwood, 1992. [I]

HOMELESSNESS

At the Sound of the Beep by Marilyn Sachs. New York: Dutton, 1990. [I]

The Beggar's Ride by Theresa Nelson. New York: Orchard/Jackson, 1992. [MS]

Dew Drop Dead by James Howe. New York: Atheneum, 1990. [I]

Fastest Friend in the West by Vicki Grove. New York: Putnam, 1990. [I]

Fly Away Home by Eve Bunting. New York: Clarion, 1991. [P]

Monkey Island by Paula Fox. New York: Orchard, 1991. [I]

Mop, Moondance, and the Nagasaki Knights by Walter Dean Myers. New York: Delacorte, 1992. [I]

No Place to Be: Voices of Homeless Children by Judith Berck. Boston: Houghton Mifflin, 1992. [MS]

Secret City, USA by Felice Holman. New York: Scribner, 1990. [MS]

Sophie and the Sidewalk Man by Stephanie S. Tolan. New York: Four Winds, 1992. [P]

Stay Tuned by Barbara Corcoran. New York: Atheneum, 1991. [MS]

Uncle Willy and the Soup Kitchen by Anne Di Salvo-Ryan. New York: Morrow, 1991. [P]

HUMAN RIGHTS

All the Lights in the Night by Arthur A. Levine. New York: Tambourine, 1991. [P]

Between Two Worlds by Jean Lingard. New York: Lodestar, 1991. [MS]

Great Lives: Human Rights by William Jay Jacobs. New York: Scribner, 1990. [I]

IMMIGRATION

Dan Thuy's New Life in America by Karen O'Connor. Minneapolis: Lerner, 1992. [I]

Ellis Island: New Hope in a New Land by William J. Jacobs. New York: Scribner, 1990. [I]

An Ellis Island Christmas by Maxinne Rhea Leighton. New York: Viking, 1992. [P]

Goodbye, Vietnam by Gloria Whelan. New York: Knopf, 1992. [I]

Illegal Aliens by Pierre N. Hausser. New York: Chelsea, 1990. [MS]

Immigrants Who Returned Home by Betty Boyd Caroli. New York: Chelsea, 1990. [MS]

Land of Hope by Joan Lowery Nixon. New York: Bantam, 1992. [I]

Leaving for America by Roslyn Bresnick-Perry. Chicago: Children's Book Press, 1992. [P]

Letters from Rifka by Karen Hesse. New York: Holt, 1992. [I]

My Grandmother's Journey by John Cech. New York: Bradbury, 1991. [P]

Our Eddie by Sulamith Ish-Kishar. New York: Knopf, 1992. [I]

A Peddler's Dream by Janice Shefelman. Boston: Houghton Mifflin, 1992. [P]

The Scottish Americans by Catherine Aman. New York: Chelsea, 1991. [I]

REFUGEES

Along the Tracks by Tamar Bergman. Boston: Houghton Mifflin, 1991. [MS]

The Clay Marble by Minfong Ho. New York: Farrar, Straus & Giroux, 1991. [MS]

Onion Tears by Diana Kidd. New York: Orchard, 1991. [I]

The Sky Is Falling by Kit Pearson. New York: Viking, 1990. [I]

Tug of War by Joan Lingard. New York: Lodestar, 1990. [MS]

SCIENCE: BATS

Amazing Bats by Frank Grennoway. New York: Knopf, 1991. [P]

Bats by Sharon Sigmond Shebar and Susan Shebar. New York: Watts, 1990. [I]

Bat Times by Ruth Horowitz. New York: Four Winds, 1991. [P]

A Promise to the Sun: An African Story by Tololwa M. Mollel. Boston: Joy Street, 1992. [P]

SCIENCE: BOTANY

The Big Tree by Bruce Hiscock. New York: Atheneum. 1991. [I]

Cactus by Carol Lerner. New York. Morrow, 1992. [P]

A Child's Book of Wildflowers by M. A. Kelly. New York: Four Winds, 1992. [I]

The Clover and the Bee: A Book of Pollination by Anne Ophelia Dowden. New York: Crowell, 1990. [MS]

Crinkleroot's Guide to Knowing the Trees by Jim Arnosky. New York: Bradbury, 1992. [P]

Dumb Cane and Daffodils: Poisonous Plants in the House and the Garden by Carol Lerner. New York: Morrow, 1990. [I]

From Seed to Plant by Gail Gibbons. New York: Holiday House, 1991. [P]

How Did We Find Out About Photosynthesis? by Isaac Asimov. New York: Walker, 1989. [I]

Succession: From Field to Forest by Willa Reed. Hillside, NJ: Enslow, 1991. [MS]

Tree of Life: The World of the African Baobab by Barbara Bush. San Francisco, CA: Sierra, 1989. [I]

Wonderful Pussy Willows by Jerome Wexler. New York: Dutton, 1992. [P]

SCIENCE: CHEMISTRY

How to Make a Chemical Volcano and Other Mysterious Experiments by Alan Kramer. New York: Watts, 1989. [I]

SCIENCE: CONSERVATION

Circle of Life Series by Alexandra Siy. New York: Dillon, 1992. [I]

Come Back, Salmon by Molly Cone. San Francisco, CA: Sierra, 1992. [I]

Coral Reefs in Danger by Christopher Lampton. Brookfield, CT: Millbrook, 1992. [I]

Dinosaurs to the Rescue by Laurie Krasny and Marie Brown. Boston: Joy Street, 1992. [P]

Earth at Risk Series by various authors. New York: Chelsea, 1991. [MS]

Earth Day by Wilma Willis Gore. Hillside, NJ: Enslow, 1992. [P]

Ecology Watch Series. Minneapolis: Dillon, 1992. [I]

Island Baby by Holly Keller. New York: Greenwillow, 1992. [P]

Junkyard Bandicoots and Other Tales of the World's Endangered Species by Joyce Rogers Wolkomir and Richard Wolkomir. New York: Wiley, 1992. [I]

The Land of the Grey Wolf by Thomas Locker. New York: Dial, 1991. [P]

Look Out for Turtles by Melvin Berger. New York: HarperCollins, 1992. [P]

Our Earth Series by Ron Hirschi. New York: Bantam, 1992. [P]

Our Endangered Planet: Life on Land by Mary Hoff and Mary M. Rodgers. Minneapolis: Lerner, 1992. [I]

Places of Refuge: Our National Wildlife Refuge System by Dorothy Hinshaw Patent. New York: Clarion, 1992. [I]

A River Ran Wild: An Environmental History by Lynn Cherry. San Diego: Gulliver, 1992. [I]

Sierra Club Book of Our National Parks by Donald Young and Cynthia Overbeak Bix. San Francisco: Sierra Club, 1990. [I]

The Turtle Watchers by Pamela Powell. New York: Viking, 1992. [I]

View from the Air: Charles Lindbergh's Earth and Sky by Reeve Lindbergh. New York: Viking, 1992. [P]

SCIENCE: CORAL REEFS

Coral Reefs by Barbara Taylor. New York: Darling, 1992. [I]

The Great Barrier Reef: A Living Laboratory by Rebecca L. Johnson. Minneapolis: Lerner, 1992. [I]

A Reef Comes to Life: Creating an Undersea Exhibit by Nat Segaloff and Paul Erickson. New York: Watts, 1991. [I]

SCIENCE: DESERT

Cactus Hotel by Brenda Z. Guiberson. New York: Holt, 1991. [P]

Desert Life by Barbara Taylor. New York: Darling, 1992. [I]

A Desert Year by Carol Lerner. New York: Morrow, 1991. [I]

A Night and Day in the Desert by Jennifer Owings Dewey. Boston: Little, Brown, 1991. [P]

Wildlife Southwest by Jill Skramstad. San Francisco: Chronicle, 1992. [I]

SCIENCE: ENDANGERED SPECIES

African Elephants: Giants of the Land by Dorothy Hinshaw Patent. New York: Holiday, 1991. [P]

And Then There Was One: The Mysteries of Extinction by Margery Facklam. Boston: Sierra/Little, Brown, 1990. [I]

Endangered Animals by Victor H. Waldrop. Vienna, VA: National Wildlife, 1990. [I]

Great Whales: The Gentle Giant by Patricia Lawler. New York: Holt, 1991. [P]

The Heiko: New Zealand's Yellow-Eyed Penquin by Adele Vernon. New York: Penguin, 1991. [I]

Humpback Whale by Michael Bright. New York: Watts, 1990. [I]

The Komodo Dragon by Susan Schafer. Minneapolis: Dillon, 1992. [I]

The Manatee by Jean H. Siebbald. Minneapolis: Dillon, 1990. [I]

Manatee: On Location by Kathy Darling. New York: Lothrop, 1991. [I]

Our Vanishing Farm Animals: Saving America's Rare Breeds by Catherine Paladino. Boston: Joy Street, 1991. [P]

An Owl in the House: A Naturalist's Diary by Bernd Heinrich. Boston: Joy Street, 1990. [I]

Panda by Caroline Arnold. New York: Morrow, 1992. [I]

Pelicans by Dorothy Hinshaw Patent. New York: Clarion, 1992. [I]

Saving Our Wildlife by Laurence Prigle. Hillside, NJ: Enslow, 1990. [I]

The Vanishing Manatee by Margaret Goff Clark. New York: Cobblehill, 1990. [I]

SCIENCE: ENVIRONMENT

Global Warming by Laurence Pringle. New York: Arcade, 1990. [I]

The Greenhouse Effect: Life on a Warmer Planet by Rebecca L. Johnson. Minneapolis: Lerner, 1990. [I]

Greening the City Streets: The Story of Community Gardens by Barbara A. Huff. New York: Clarion, 1990. [I]

Just a Dream by Chris Van Allsburg. Boston: Houghton Mifflin, 1990. [P/I]

My First Green Book by Angela Wilkes. New York: Knopf, 1991. [I]

SCIENCE: FLIGHT

Adventures in Space Series by Susan Dudley Gold. New York: Crestwood, 1992. [I]

Amelia Earhart: Flying for Adventure by Mary Wade. Brookfield, CT: Millbrook, 1992. [I]

Before the Wright Brothers by Don Berliner. Minneapolis: Lerner, 1990. [I]

The Big Balloon Race by Eleanor Coerr. New York: Colliers, 1992. [P]

Breaking the Sound Barrier by Nathan Aasing. New York: Messner, 1992. [I]

Charles Lindbergh by Blythe Randolph. New York: Watts, 1990. [MS]

Eureka! It's an Airplane! by Jeanne Bendick. Brookfield, CT: Millbrook, 1992. [I]

Flight: The Journey of Charles Lindbergh by Robert Burleigh. New York: Philomel, 1991. [P]

Fly the Hot Ones by Steven Lindlelom. Boston: Houghton Mifflin, 1991. [I]

SCIENCE: FOREST

The Gift of a Tree by Alvin Tresselt. New York: Lothrop, 1992. [P]

How the Forest Grew by William Jaspersohn. New York: Greenwillow, 1989. [I]

Once There Was a Tree by Natalia Romanova. New York: Doubleday, 1985. [I]

Summer of the Fire: Yellowstone by Patricia Lauber. New York: Orchard, 1991. [I]

Temperate Forests by Basil Booth. New York: Burdett, 1989. [I]

Tree Trunk Traffic by Bianca Lavies. New York: Dutton, 1989. [P]

The Tremendous Tree Book by Barbara Brenner and Mary Garelick. Jonesdale, PA: Caroline, 1992. [P]

SCIENCE: GALAPAGOS ISLANDS

Dawn to Dusk in the Galapagos: Flightless Birds, Swimming Lizards, and Other Fascinating Creatures by Rita Golden Gelman. Boston: Little, Brown, 1991. [I]

Galapagos Tortoise by Susan Schafer. New York: Dillon, 1992. [I/MS]

Swimming with the Sea Lions and Other Adventures in the Galapagos Islands by Ann McGovern. New York: Scholastic, 1992. [I]

SCIENCE: GEOLOGY

Earth Alive! by Sandra Markle. New York: Lothrop, 1991. [I]

Natural Wonders and Disasters by Billy Goodman. Boston: Little, Brown, 1991. [I]

SCIENCE: INVENTORS AND INVENTIONS

Great Lives: Inventions and Technology by Milton Lomask. New York: Scribner, 1991. [I]

Inventions by Lionel Bender. New York: Knopf, 1991. [I]

Mistakes That Worked by Charlotte Faltz Jones. New York: Doubleday, 1991. [I]

SCIENCE: LIFE CYCLES

The Atlantic Salmon by Bianca Lavies. New York: Dutton, 1992.

Growing Up by Sarah Waters. New York: Dial, 1992. [P]

Ladybug by Emery Bernard. New York: Holiday, 1992. [P]

Lamb by Gordon Clayton. New York: Lodestar, 1992. [P]

The Life and Times of the Apple by Charles Micucci. New York: Orchard, 1992. [P]

Monarch Butterflies: Mysterious Travelers by Bianca Lavies. New York: Dutton, 1992. [I]

Mouse by Barrie Watts. New York: Lodestar, 1992. [P]

SCIENCE: NATURAL DISASTERS

Born of Fire: Volcanoes and Igneous Rocks by Robert I. Tilling. Hillside, NJ: Enslow, 1991. [MS]

Come a Tide by George Ella Lyon. New York: Orchard/Jackson, 1990. [P]

Disaster Series (Blizzards, Earthquakes, Forest Fires, Hurricanes, Tornadoes, Volcanoes) by Christopher Lampton. Brookfield, CT: Millbrook, 1991. [I]

Earthquakes by Franklyn M. Branley. New York: Crowell, 1990. [P]

Earthquakes by Seymour Simon. New York: Morrow, 1991. [I]

Earthquake and Volcano by Basil Booth. New York: Simon, 1992. [MS]

Glaciers: Ice on the Move by Sally M. Walker. Minneapolis: Carolrhoda, 1990. [I]

The Great Yellowstone Fire by Carole Garbuny Vogel and Katheryn Allen Goldner. San Francisco: Sierra Club, 1990. [I]

Volcanoes and Earthquakes by Susanna Van Rose. New York: Knopf, 1992. [I]

Yellowstone Fires: Flames and Rebirth by Dorothy Hishaw. New York: Holiday House, 1990. [I]

SCIENCE: OCEANOGRAPHY

Alligators to Zooplankton: A Dictionary of Water Babies by Les Kaufman. New York: Watts, 1991. [I]

The Atlantic Salmon by Bianca Lavies. New York: Dutton, 1992. [I]

Beneath the Waves: Exploring the Hidden World of the Kelp Forest by Norbert Nu. San Francisco: Chronicle, 1992. [I]

Diving into Darkness: A Submersible Explores the Sea by Rebecca L. Johnson. Minneapolis: Lerner, 1989. [MS]

Do Fishes Get Thirsty? by Les Kaufman. New York: Watts, 1991. [I]

Life in a Tidal Pool by Alvin Silverstein and Virginia Silverstein. Boston: Little, Brown, 1990. [I]

Our Endangered Planet: Oceans by Mary Hoff and Mary M. Rodgers. Minneapolis: Lerner, 1992. [I]

Seashore by Steve Parker. New York: Knopf, 1989. [MS]

Sharks and Other Creatures of the Deep by Philip Steele. Minneapolis: Dillon, 1991. [I]

Under the Sea from A–Z by Anne Doubilet. New York: Crown, 1991. [P]

Waterman's Boy by Susan Sharpe. New York: Bradbury, 1990. [I]

Windows on Wildlife by Ginny Johnston and Judy Cutchins. New York: Morrow, 1990. [I]

SCIENCE: OUTER SPACE

Adventures in Space Series by Susan Dudley Gold. New York: Crestwood, 1992. [I]

Astronaut Training Book for Kids by Kim Long. New York: Lodestar, 1990. [I]

Mercury by Seymour Simon. New York: Simon, 1992. [I]

Small Worlds: Sixty Moons of Our Solar System by Joseph W. Kelch. New York: Messner, 1990. [MS]

The Space Shuttle by George Fichter. New York: Watts, 1990. [I]

Voyager: An Adventure to the Edge of the Solar System by Sally Ride and Tom O'Shaughnessy. New York: Crown, 1992. [I]

The World's Space Programs by Isaac Asimov. Milwaukee: Gareth Stevens, 1990. [I]

SCIENCE: RAIN FORESTS

The Great Kapok Tree: A Tale of the Amazon Rain Forest by Lynne Cherry. San Diego: Harcourt Brace Jovanovich, 1990. [P]

Jungle Rescue: Saving the New World Tropical Rain Forests by Christina G. Miller and Louise A. Berry. New York: Atheneum, 1991. [I]

One Day in the Tropical Rain Forest by Jean Craighead George. New York: Crowell, 1990. [I]

Welcome to the Green House by Jane Yolen. New York: Putnam, 1993. [P]

SCIENCE: RECYCLING

Cartons, Cans, and Orange Peels by Joanna Foster. New York: Clarion, 1991. [I]

Recycle! A Handbook for Kids by Gail Gibbons. Boston: Little, Brown, 1992. [P]

Recycling by Rebecca Stefoff. New York: Chelsea, 1991. [MS]

SCIENCE: SOLAR SYSTEM

Astronomy by Dennis Fradin. Chicago: Children's Press, 1987. [I/MS]

Eclipse by Franklyn Branley. New York: HarperCollins, 1988. [P]

Galileo by Leonard Everett Fisher. New York: Macmillan, 1992. [I]

How Did We Find Out About Neptune? by Isaac Asimov. New York: Walker, 1990. [I/MS]

If You Lived on Mars by Melvin Berger. New York: Lodestar, 1988. [I/MS]

Journey to the Planets by Patricia Lauber. New York: Crown, 1990. [I/MS]

The Magic School Bus, Lost in the Solar System by Joanna Cole. New York: Scholastic, 1990. [P]

Mercury by Seymour Simon. New York: Morrow, 1992. [P/I/MS]

The Moon Seems to Change by Franklyn Branley. New York: HarperCollins, 1987. [P]

Mysteries of the Planets by Franklyn Branley. New York: Dutton, 1987. [I/MS]

Our Solar System by Seymour Simon. New York: Morrow, 1992. [P/I/MS]

Seeing Earth from Space by Patricia Lauber. New York: Orchard, 1990. [I/MS]

Shooting Stars by Franklyn Branley. New York: HarperCollins, 1989. [P]

Space Words: A Dictionary by Seymour Simon. New York: HarperCollins, 1991. [P]

The Sun: Our Nearest Star by Franklyn Branley. New York: HarperCollins, 1988. [P]

Uranus: The Seventh Planet by Franklyn Branley. New York: HarperCollins, 1988. [I/MS]

Venus by Muriel Schloss. New York: Watts, 1991. [I/MS]

Voyager to the Planets by Necia Apfel. New York: Clarion, 1991. [I/MS]

Voyagers from Space by Patricia Lauber. New York: HarperCollins, 1989. [I/MS]

SCIENCE: WATER

Amazon by Peter Laurie. Honesdale, PA: Caroline, 1992. [P]

Follow the Water from Brook to Ocean by Arthur Dorros. New York: HarperCollins, 1991. [P]

Hudson River by Peter Lourie. Honesdale, PA: Boyds Mill Press, 1991. [I]

River Keeper by George Ancona. New York: Macmillan, 1990. [I]

River Rats by Carolyn Stevermer. San Diego: Harcourt Brace Jovanovich, 1992. [I]

The Stream by Naomi Russell. New York: Dutton, 1991. [P]

Water Up, Water Down: The Hydrologic Cycle by Sally M. Walker. Minneapolis: Carolrhoda, 1992. [I]

Water's Way by Lisa Westberg Peters. New York: Arcade, 1991. [P]

Wings Along the Waterway by Mary Barrett Brown. New York: Orchard, 1992. [I]

World Water Watch by Michelle Koch. New York: Greenwillow, 1993. [P]

Yukon River by Peter Lourie. Honesdale, PA: Boyds Mill Press, 1992. [I]

SCIENCE: WEATHER

Powerful Waves by D. M. Souza. Minneapolis: Carolrhoda, 1992. [I]

Sierra Club Book of Weather Wisdom by Vicki McVey. San Francisco: Sierra, 1991. [I]

The Weather Sky by Bruce McMillan. New York: Farrar, Straus & Giroux, 1991. [I]

Weather Words and What They Mean by Gail Gibbons. New York: Holiday House, 1990. [P]

What Will the Weather Be Like Today? by Paul Rogers. New York: Greenwillow, 1990. [P]

SCIENCE: ZOOLOGY

Animal Architecture by Jennifer Owings Dewey. New York: Orchard, 1991. [I]

Primates in the Zoo by Roland Smith. Brookfield, CT: Millbrook, 1992. [I]

Zoo Animals by Philip Dowell and Jerry Young. New York: Alladin, 1991. [P]

SENIOR CITIZENS

Blow Me a Kiss, Miss Lilly by Nancy White Carlstrom. New York: Harper and Row 1990. [P]

Grandpa's Song by Tony Johnston. New York: Dial, 1991. [P]

The Keepsake Chest by Katherine Wilson Precek. New York: Macmillan, 1992. [MS]

Old John by Peter Hartling. New York: Lothrop, Lee, and Shepard, 1990. [I]

This Quiet Lady by Charlotte Zolotow. New York: Greenwillow, 1992. [P]

UNITED STATES EXPLORERS

Against All Opposition: Black Explorers in America by Jim Haskins. New York: Walker, 1992. [I]

Encounter by Jane Yolen. San Diego: Harcourt Brace Jovanovich, 1992. [I]

Explorers and Mapmakers by Peter Ryan. New York: Lodestar, 1990. [I]

Follow the Dream by Peter Sis. New York: Knopf, 1991. [P]

Last Stand at the Alamo by Alden R. Carter. New York: Watts, 1990. [P]

The Lewis and Clark Expedition by Patrick McGrath. New York: Burdett, 1992. [I]

The Remarkable Voyages of Captain Cook by Rhonda Blumberg. New York: Bradbury, 1991. [I]

Zebulon Pike and the Explorers of the American Southwest by Jared Stallones. New York: Chelsea, 1991. [MS]

WOMEN

American Women of Achievement Series. New York: Chelsea, 1990. [MS]

Jane Goodall: Friend of the Chimps by Eileen Lucas. Brookfield, CT: Millbrook, 1992. [I]

Letters from a Slave Girl: The Story of Harriet Jacobs by Mary E. Lyons. New York: Scribner, 1992. [MS]

A Long Way to Go by Libby O'Neal. New York: Viking, 1990. [I]

Rachel Carson: Voice for the Earth by Ginger Wadsworth. Minneapolis: Lerner, 1992. [I]

Sojourner Truth: Ain't I a Woman? by Patricia McKissack and Frederick McKissack. New York: Scholastic, 1992. [I]

Visions: Stories About Women Artists by Leslie Sills. New York: Albert Whitman, 1993. [I]

A Whole New Ball Game: The Story of the All-American Girls Professional Baseball League by Sue Macy. Boston: Holt, 1993. [MS]

In cooperative projects the Children's Book Council, the National Science Teachers Association, and the National Council for the Social Studies annually publish bibliographies of outstanding books during the year. Their annotated bibliographies are rich resources for TI teachers. "Outstanding Science Trade Books for Children (Grades K–8)" appears in the March issue of *Science and Children.* "Notable Children's Trade Books in the Field of Social Studies" is published in the April/May issue of *Social Education.*

Resource Section
Magazines for Student Research

NAME	ORDERING ADDRESS	SUBJECT	LEVEL
Boy's Life	Boy's Life Subscription 1325 Walnut Hill Lane Irving, TX 75015-2079	General	P/I
Chickadee Magazine	P.O. Box 11314 Des Moines, IA 50340	Science/ Nature	P
Child Life	P.O. Box 10003 Des Moines, IA 50340	General	P/I
Children's Digest	P.O. Box 10003 Des Moines, IA 50340	General	MS
Children's Playmate	P.O. Box 10003 Des Moines, IA 50340	General	P
Classical Calliope	Cobblestone Publications 30 Grove St. Peterborough, NH 03458	Ancient West. Civ./ The Classics	I/MS
Cobblestone	Cobblestone Publications 30 Grove St. Peterborough, NH 03458	American History	I/MS

P = Primary
I = Intermediate
MS = Middle School

NAME	ORDERING ADDRESS	SUBJECT	LEVEL
Current Events	Current Events Field Publications 4343 Equity Drive P.O. Box 16630 Columbus, OH 43216	News	MS
Current Health I	Field Publications 4343 Equity Dr. P.O. Box 16630 Columbus, OH 43216	Health Ed.	I/MS
Current Science	Field Publications 4343 Equity Dr. P.O. Box 16630 Columbus, OH 43216	Science	I/MS
Dolphin Log	The Cousteau Society 930 W. 21 St. Norfolk, VA 23517	Science	MS
Faces	Cobblestone Publications 30 Grove St. Peterborough, NH 03458	World Cultures	I/MS
Highlights for Children	P.O. Box 269 Columbus, OH 43272-0002	General	P/I
Images of Excellence	Images of Excellence Foundation P.O. Box 1131 Boiling Springs, NC 28017	Social Studies	I/MS
Jack and Jill	P.O. Box 10003 Des Moines, IA 50340	General	P
Junior Scholastic	2931 E. McCarthy St. P.O. Box 3710 Jefferson City, MO 65102-9957	Social Studies	MS
Kid City	200 Watt Street P.O. Box 2924 Bouler, CO 80322	General	P/I
Kind News	Box 362 East Haddam, CT 06423	Creatures/ Environment	P/I
Koala Club News	San Diego Zoo Membership Department P.O. Box 271 San Diego, CA 92112	Animals	All

RESOURCE SECTION C

NAME	ORDERING ADDRESS	SUBJECT	LEVEL
National Geographic World	P.O. Box 2330 Washington, DC 20077-9955	Natural History, Science, and Outdoors	All
Odyssey	Nancy Mack Odyssey 1027 N. Seventh St. Milwaukee, WI 53233	Space and Astronomy	All
Owl Magazine	P.O. Box 11314 Des Moines, IA 50340	Science and Nature	I/MS
Ranger Rick	Membership National Wildlife Fed. 8925 Leesburg Pike Vienna, VA 22180-0001	Nature	All
Scholastic News	Scholastic 2931 E. McCarty St. Jefferson City, MO 65102-9957	Current Events	P/I
Scholastic Search	Scholastic 2931 E. McCarty St. Jefferson City, MO 65102-9957	Social Studies	I/MS
Scholastic Update	Scholastic 2931 E. McCarty St. Jefferson City, MO 65102-9957	Language Arts	I/MS
Science Weekly	Subscription Dept. 2141 Industrial Pkwy. Silver Spring, MD 20904	Science	All
Scienceland	501 Fifth Avenue New York, NY 10017-6165	Science	P
Science World	Scholastic 2931 E. McCarty St. Jefferson City, MO 65102-9957	Science	MS
Skipping Stones: A Multi-Ethnic Children's Forum	80574 Hazelton Road Cottage Grove, OR 97424	Culture/ Environment	All
SuperScience Red Edition	Scholastic 2931 E. McCarty St. Jefferson City, MO 65102-9957	Science	P

NAME	ORDERING ADDRESS	SUBJECT	LEVEL
SuperScience Blue Edition	Scholastic 2931 E. McCarty St. Jefferson City, MO 65102-9957	Science	I
3-2-1 Contact	P.O. Box 53051 Boulder, CO 80322-53051	Science Technology	I/MS
U*S* Kids	Field Publications 4343 Equity Drive P.O. Box 16630 Columbus, OH 43216	Real World	P/I
Weekly Reader	Field Publications 4343 Equity Drive P.O. Box 16630 Columbus, OH 43216	News	All
World Newsmap	Field Publications 4343 Equity Drive P.O. Box 16630 Columbus, OH 43216	English/ Journalism	All
Your Big Backyard	National Wildlife Federation 8925 Leesburg Pike Vienna, VA 22180	Animals & Conservation	P
Zoobooks	3590 Kettner Blvd. San Diego, CA 92101	Wildlife	All

Resource Section
Suggestions for Family and Community History Theme Immersions

FAMILY HISTORY

Questions Students Might Ask When Interviewing Family Members

- Where did you live when you were little?
- Was it in the city or the country?
- What was life like when you were little?
- How many were there in your family? (If there were brothers or sisters were you older or younger?)
- Did any other relatives live near you?
- How is life today different from when you were little?
- How are the clothes different?
- What did you use for transportation?
- Did you have to pay taxes?
- What did you do for fun?
- What games did you play?
- Were holidays celebrated in the same way they are today?
- Do you have any special family holiday recipes or menus I could copy?
- What was life like for your mother?
- What was life like for your father?
- Were schools the same?
- What was the happiest time of your childhood?
- What would you like to tell me that I haven't already asked?
- Do you have any newspaper clippings about funerals or wedding announcements I could photocopy?
- Do you remember favorite books or poems of family members?

- Are there any old books or diaries that I could see?
- What do you know about your ancestors?
- Did you know your great-grandparents or great-uncles or aunts?
- Did they tell you any stories about life when they were growing up?
- Are there any special things you can remember, such as the way they dressed, the way they spoke, the things they liked to eat, how they made their living, what their homes looked like, etc.?
- If they came from another country or another part of the United States, did they talk about it?
- If they moved either from another country or another part of the United States, did they talk about how they traveled?
- Can you think of anything else that might help me know more about our family?

Publishing of Family Histories by Students

- Booklets with lists of favorite books of family members
- Collections of favorite poetry of family members
- Collections of traditional holiday meals with recipes
- Descriptions of family holiday customs
- Descriptions of weddings and funerals of ancestors
- Lists of favorite hobbies of family members
- Taped interviews (oral history of older living relative)

Community History

Research Activities for Exploring Community History

- Read, photocopy, and summarize documents from individuals, libraries, and museums
- Locate and read published histories about the community, citizens, and historic sites
- Develop a community time line
- Locate and read books and poems written by local authors and poets (families can read the texts orally as an activity)
- Locate legends, folklore, folk songs, ghost stories, etc. from the area
- Read Native American literature from the area
- Locate the works of local artists on public display in a museum, library, or other public building
- Study old newspapers: wages listed in want ads, car prices, livestock prices, old recipes, farm and business sales, obituaries, wedding and anniversary announcements, wanted posters, fashions, home remedies advertisements, recreational opportunities such as fairs, circuses, and movies, farmer's advice, such as when to plant potatoes, astronomy, church news, and community celebrations

- Visit historical places: old buildings such as courthouses, churches, houses, and banks; archives for the local and state area, including a review of old photographs, letters, diaries, military papers, census records, and WPA histories; battlegrounds; and cemetery tombstones and epitaphs
- Study a cemetery by examining dates on tombstones, family names (especially names that are not common today), birthplaces, length of lives (looking for patterns such as epidemics that caused deaths of a large number of people and noting the number of infant fatalities), epitaphs, shapes and styles of tombstones, placement of cemetery, number of cemeteries in the area, and size of cemetery

Resource Section
Selected Addresses for Theme Immersion Information

E

NATIONAL GOVERNMENT ADDRESSES

Commission on Civil Rights
1121 Vermont Avenue NW
Washington, DC 20425

Department of Agriculture
The Mall, 12th & 14th Streets
Washington, DC 20250

Department of Commerce
14th Street
Washington, DC 20230

Department of Defense
The Pentagon
Washington, DC 20301

Department of Education
400 Maryland Avenue SW
Washington, DC 20202

Department of Energy
1000 Independence Avenue SW
Washington, DC 20585

Department of Health and
Human Services
200 Independence Avenue SW
Washington, DC 20201

Department of Housing & Urban
Development
451 7th Street SW
Washington, DC 20410

Department of the Interior
C Street Between 18th & 19th
Streets
Washington, DC 20240

Department of Justice
Constitution Avenue and 10th
Street NW
Washington, DC 20530

Department of Labor
200 Constitution Avenue NW
Washington, DC 20210

Department of State
2201 C Street NW
Washington, DC 20520

Department of Transportation
400 17th Street SW
Washington, DC 20590

Department of the Treasury
1500 Pennsylvania Avenue NW
Washington, DC 20220

Environmental Protection Agency
401 M Street NW
Washington, DC 20460

Export-Import Bank of the United
States
811 Vermont Avenue NW
Washington, DC 20571

Federal Maritime Commission
1100 L Street NW
Washington, DC 20573

Government Printing Office
North Capitol & H Streets NW
Washington, DC 20401

Library of Congress
101 Independence Avenue SE
Washington, DC 20540

National Aeronautics & Space
Administration
600 Independence Avenue SW
Washington, DC 20546

National Archives & Records
Administration
7th Street & Pennsylvania Avenue
Washington, DC 20408

National Foundation on the Arts &
Humanities
1100 Pennsylvania Avenue NW
Washington, DC 20506

National Science Foundation
1800 G Street NW
Washington, DC 20550

Peace Corps
1990 K Street NW
Washington, DC 20526

United States Postal Service
475 L'Enfant Plaza SW
Washington, DC 20260

The White House Staff
1600 Pennsylvania Avenue NW
Washington, DC 20500

NATIONAL ORGANIZATION ADDRESSES

Aeronautics Association
1815 N. Fort Myer Drive
Arlington, VA 22209

Air Pollution Control Association
P.O. Box 2861
Pittsburgh, PA 15230

Air and Waste Management
P.O. Box 2861
Pittsburgh, PA 15230

American Association for the Study
of Afro-American Life and History
1401 14th Street NW
Washington, DC 20005

American Association of Zoological
Parks & Aquariums
Oglebay Park
Wheeling, WV 26003

American Cancer Society
90 Park Avenue
New York, NY 10017

American Diabetes Association
1660 Duke Street
Alexandria, VA 22314

American Forestry Association
1516 P Street NW
Washington, DC 20005

American Foundation for the Blind
15 W. 16th Street
New York, NY 10011

American Heart Association
7320 Greenville Avenue
Dallas, TX 75231

American Institute of Nutrition
9650 Rockville Pike
Bethesda, MD 20814

American Lung Association
1740 Broadway
New York, NY 10019

American Society for Prevention of
Cruelty to Animals
441 East 92nd Street
New York, NY 10128

Americans for Human Rights and
Social Justice
P.o. Box 6258
Ft. Worth, TX 76115

Animal Welfare Institute
P.O. Box 3650
Washington, DC 20007

Association on American Indian
Affairs
245 Fifth Avenue
Suite 1801
New York, NY 10016-8728

Association of Multiethnic
Americans
1060 Tennessee Street
San Francisco, CA 94107

Bread for the World
802 Rhode Island Avenue NE
Washington, DC 20018

Clean Energy Research Institute
1251 Memorial Drive
219 MacArthur Engineering
Building
Coral Gables, FL 33146

Congress of Racial Equality
1457 Flatbush Avenue
Brooklyn, NY 11210

Council on Foreign Relations
59 E. 66th Street
New York, NY 10021

Defenders of Wildlife
1244 19th Street NW
Washington, DC 20036

Federation of the Handicapped
211 W 14th Street
New York, NY 10011

Freedoms Foundation at Valley
Forge
Valley Forge, PA 1948!

The Fund for Animals
200 W. 57th Street
New York, NY 10019

Humane Society of the U.S.
2100 L Street NW
Washington, DC 20037

International Association of
Pollution Control
444 N. Capitol Street NW
Washington, DC 20001

NAACP
4805 Mt. Hope Drive
Baltimore, MD 21215

National Association of Arab
Americans
2033 M Street NW
Washington, DC 20036

National Association of the Deaf
814 Thayer Avenue
Silver Springs, MO 20910

National Association of the
Physically Handicapped
440 Lafayette Avenue
Cincinnati, OH 45220-1000

National Audubon Society
950 Third Avenue
New York, NY 10022

National Multiple Sclerosis Society
733 Third Avenue
New York, NY 10017

National Recycling Coalition
1101 30th Street NW
Washington, DC 20007

National Wildlife Federation
1400 16th Street NW
Washington, DC 20036

Nature Conservancy
1815 N. Lynn Street
Arlington, VA 22209

The Naturist Society
P.O. Box 132
Oshkosh, WI 54902

Society of America Leukemia
733 Third Avenue
New York, NY 10017

United Cerebral Palsy Association
7 Penn Plaza
New York, NY 10001

United States Olympic Committee
1750 E. Boulder Street
Colorado Springs, CO 80909

United States Space Education
Association
745 Turnpike Road
Elizabethtown, PA 17022

Water Environment Federation
601 Wythe Street
Alexandria, VA 22314

Wilderness Society
900 17th Street NW
Washington, DC 20006

World Wildlife Fund
1250 19th Street NW
Washington, DC 20037

STATE GOVERNMENT

Alabama Business Council
P.O. Box 76
Montgomery, Al 36195
(1-800-392-8096)

Alaska Division of Tourism
P.O. Box 110801
Juneau, AK 99811-0801
(1-907-465-2010)

Arizona Tourist Information
1480 East Bethany Home Road
Suite 180
Phoenix, AZ 85014
(1-602-254-6500)

Arkansas Chamber of Commerce
One Spring Building
Little Rock, AR 72201-2486
(1-800-NATURAL)

California Chamber of Commerce
1201 K Street
Sacramento, CA 95814
(1-800-862-2543)

Colorado Tourist Information
5500 Syracuse Circle
Suite 267
Englewood, CO 80111
(1-800-433-2656)

Connecticut Tourist Information
865 Brook Street
Rocky Hill, CT 06067
(1-800-CT-BOUND)

Delaware Chamber of Commerce
One Commerce Center
Wilmington, DE 19801
(1-800-441-8846)

Florida Tourist Information
126 Van Buren Street
Tallahassee, FL 32399-2000
(1-904-487-1462)

Georgia Chamber of Commerce
235 International Boulevard
Atlanta, GA 30303
(1-800-VISIT GA)

Hawaii Chamber of Commerce
Dillingham Building
735 Bishop Street
Honolulu, HI 96813
(1-808-545-4300)

Idaho Tourist Information
700 W. State Street
Boise, ID 83720
(1-800-635-7820)

Illinois Tourist Information
620 E. Adams Street
Springfield, IL 62701
(1-800-223-0121)

Indiana Chamber of Commerce
One North Capital, Suite 200
Indianapolis, IN 46204
(1-800-289-6646)

Iowa Tourist Information
200 E. Grand Avenue
Des Moines, IA 50309
(1-800-345-IOWA)

Kansas Tourist Information
400 SW 8th Street
5th Floor
Topeka, KS 66603
(1-800-2KANSAS)

Kentucky Chamber of Commerce
452 Versailles Road
Frankfort, KY 40602
(1-800-225-TRIP)

Louisiana Tourist Information
P.O. Box 94291
Baton Rouge, LA 70804
(1-800-33-GUMBO)

Maine Chamber of Commerce
126 Sewall Street
Augusta, ME 04330
(1-800-533-9595)

Maryland Chamber of Commerce
111 S. Calvert Street
Baltimore, MD 21202
(1-800-543-1036)

Massachusetts Tourist Information
100 Cambridge Street
Boston, MA 02202
(1-800-624-MASS)

Michigan Chamber of Commerce
200 N. Washington Square
Lansing, MI 48933
(1-800-543-2937)

Minnesota Tourist Information
375 Jackson Street
St. Paul, MN 55101
(1-800-328-1461)

Mississippi Department of
Economics
P.O. Box 1849
Jackson, MS 39205
(1-800-647-2290)

Missouri Chamber of Commerce
400 E. High Street
Jefferson City, MO 65101
(1-800-877-1234)

Montana Chamber of Commerce
2030 11th Avenue
Helena, MT 59624
(1-800-541-1447)

Nebraska Chamber of Commerce
1320 Lincoln Mall
Lincoln, NE 68501
(1-800-228-4307)

Nevada Tourist Information
Capitol Complex
Carson City, NV 89710
(1-800-638-2328)

New Hampshire Tourist Information
P.O. Box 856
Concord, NH 03302-0856
(1-800-271-2666)

New Jersey Chamber of Commerce
51 Commerce Street
Newark, NJ 07102
(1-800-JERSEY-7)

New Mexico Tourist Information
P.O. Box 20003
Sante Fe, NM 87503
(1-800-545-2040)

New York Tourist Information
1 Commerce Street
Albany, NY 12245
(1-800-CALLNYS)

North Carolina Tourist
480 N. Salisbury Street
Raleigh, NC 27603
(1-800-VISITNC)

North Dakota Chamber of
Commerce
P.O. Box 2467
Fargo, ND 58108
(1-800-437-2077)

Ohio Chamber of Commerce
35 E. Gay Street
Columbus, OH 43215
(1-800-BUCKEYE)

Oklahoma Chamber of Commerce
4020 N. Lincoln Boulevard
Oklahoma City, OK 73105
(1-800-652-6552)

Oregon Tourist Information
775 Summer Street NE
Salem, OR 97310
(1-800-547-7842)

Pennsylvania Chamber of
Commerce
222 N. 3rd Street
Harrisburg, PA 17101
(1-800-VISITPA)

Rhode Island Chamber of
Commerce
30 Exchange Terrace
Providence, RI 02908
(1-800-556-2484)

South Carolina Tourist Information
930 Richland Street
Columbia, SC 29201
(1-803-734-0122)

South Dakota Tourist Information
711 E. Wells Avenue
Pierre, SD 57501-3369
(1-800-843-1930)

Tennessee Tourist Information
5th Fl. Rachel Jackson Building
Nashville, TN 37219
(1-615-741-2158)

Texas Chamber of Commerce
900 Congress
Suite 501
Austin, TX 78701
(1-512-472-1594)

Utah Tourist Information
Council Hall
Salt Lake City, UT 84114
(1-801-521-2822)

Vermont Tourist Information
134 State Street
Montpelier, VT 05602
(1-800-837-6668)

Virginia Chamber of Commerce
9 South Fifth Street
Richmond, VA 23219
(1-800-VISITVA)

Washington Tourist Information
P.O. Box 658
Olympia, WA 98507
(1-800-544-1800)

West Virginia Tourist Information
State Capitol
Charleston, WV 25305
(1-800-CALLWVA)

Wisconsin Tourist Information
123 W. Washington Avenue
Madison, WI 53702
(1-800-372-2737)

Wyoming Tourist Information
Etchepare Circle
Cheyenne, WY 82002
(1-800-CALLWYO)